WALKING WITH GOD

PRAYING THROUGH FOOTWORK METAPHORS IN SCRIPTURE

TERESA SANDHU

WESTBOW°
PRESS
A DIVISION OF THOMAS NELSON
& ZONDERVAN

WestBow Press books may be ordered through booksellers or by contacting:

WestBow Press
A Division of Thomas Nelson & Zondervan
1663 Liberty Drive
Bloomington, IN 47403
www.westbowpress.com
1 (866) 928-1240

ISBN: 978-1-4908-3506-8 (sc)
ISBN: 978-1-4908-3507-5 (e)

Library of Congress Control Number: 2014907456

Printed in the United States of America.

WestBow Press rev. date: 5/15/2014

Contents

Dedication

To those who desire a deep inward walk with Jesus Christ.
And, especially to those in the underground church across the
world, whose inner walk must bring great joy to our Lord.

Acknowledgements

WITH DEEP GRATITUDE to my loving husband Paul, my talented mother Doreen, and friends Grace, Diane, Roz, and Lila as well as cousin Carol for encouraging me to write. To my heart-strong children: Tej (Andrea), Kellan, and Tristan (Rebekah) for their love and technical support. To friends in our city and in different countries who embrace us as family.

To Reverend Stephanie Douglas Bowman and Audrey Dorsch for kind and invaluable mentoring and editing. Special thanks to Zora Zoretich for permission to use her idea for the cover.

To the Body of Christ for my spiritual formation: St. Dunstan's Catholic Church- Woking UK, Holy Cross Catholic Church- Deerfield IL, Christ Church - Lake Forest IL, Community Bible Study - Lake Forest IL and Mississauga ON, Bible Study Fellowship- Oakville ON, Chartwell Baptist Church- Mississauga ON, 'Barb, Irene and Janna's kitchen table Messianic Bible Study Group', Transformation Prayer Ministry, Elisha intercessory group, Aces prayer and celebration group, Little Trinity Anglican Church, Toronto ON, and Hanne, my prayer-walking partner.

To Sharon, Melaku, Josi, and Sister Tebebe for their inspiring, selfless service in Ethiopia.

To the authors I love: Andrew Murray, A.W. Tozer, Tim Keller, and Graham Cooke.

But mostly, I acknowledge that the Holy Spirit enables me, walking and talking with me even now.

Preface ... Why feet?

Ten years ago, feet would not have aroused my curiosity. I have no foot fetishes or serious ailments, and am not particularly ticklish. I do own a staggering number of shoes, but so do most North American women. I have never been to a reflexologist, and I didn't particularly enjoy the one time I had a pedicure. I am not the perfect candidate to write a book about feet, by most standards.

Then God set me on a new track. I had been a city intercessor with the ecumenical Elisha group in Mississauga, Ontario, for a few years. I loved seeing God's work under way in our city and enjoyed praying alongside others. As this passion grew, I attended "city prayer" seminars and read books on what God was doing in other cities around the world. What struck me, as I researched, were the breakthroughs that Argentineans made by "prayer walking" their city streets. They took Romans 16:20 as their inspiration: "The God of peace will soon crush Satan under your feet." These Christians understood the promise in the metaphor and acted on it literally. This verse and the notion of feet and faith in motion together whet my interest in feet. Soon enough I was tripping over footwork metaphors everywhere and asking the Holy Spirit for insight. Could these metaphors teach me how to walk with God?

Before long I had collected and catalogued hundreds of biblical footwork verses. Many captivated me by their gentle bidding and others were like sirens, warning me of danger. The one that declared the Lord's blessing on my collection was clear: "How beautiful on the mountains are the feet of the messenger who brings good news" (Isaiah 52:7, NLT). God sees our feet differently than we do. I wanted to know His perspective and His plans for the lowest member of our bodies.

I extended my research into the physical, cultural, and spiritual aspects of feet. I was like a prospector looking for gold. A lot of information is simply factual, but there is much that is symbolic:

- the "red carpet" treatment of celebrities and its classical Greek origins
- the youth gangs who declare territory with running shoes strung over electric wires
- the ancient Roman and Egyptian tradition of writing the names of enemies on the soles of their sandals so that they could literally step on them
- the Jews' becoming "the feet of the Torah" in a ritualistic dance

It was, however, the historical practice of foot binding in China that set fire to my quest. I had a visceral reaction to this vile treatment. Little girls, from the age of five, endured years of excruciating pain as their tightly bound feet became increasingly more stunted and deformed. "Violence makes the feet sacred" was the cultural maxim. In fact, the girls were immobilized. Many lost their use of language due to the pain. I came to understand that the destruction of feet is one of the plans of God's adversary. There was so much more to this topic than I had first thought. I started to investigate the depth and breadth of footwork metaphors, I found a lot of negative and positive parallels; feet deliver mixed messages.

Many Christian books introduce footwork metaphors into their themes or chapter headings. I have a shelf full of books that talk about dancing, detours, dusty feet, following, footsteps, gaining ground, paths, sitting at the feet, treading – and, of course, walking. But few offer anything beyond a brief examination of the footwork metaphor or help you bring the metaphor to life. *Walking with God* is the first book to do this.

Feet are vehicles for storytelling. Who can forget the shoes thrown at President George W. Bush by the Iraqi journalist? You may not remember the angry words he shouted, but you won't forget the shoes. In fact, there were calls throughout the Middle East at that time to have that pair of size ten shoes enshrined in an Iraqi museum as a symbol of protest. Later, joint USA and Iraqi security forces destroyed the shoes in one of the more unusual strikes in the annals of military history. That journalist's protest gained global attention because he used a powerful, universal metaphor. Feet deliver messages.

In the English language, metaphors of feet, footwear, or footwork are a part of the working vocabulary.

- When companies are environmentally conscious, they calculate the weight of their "carbon footprints."
- When armies describe the scale of their activity, they count "boots on the ground."
- When you "toe the line," you obey rules.
- When you replace someone in a position, you "step into her shoes."

Not surprisingly, we also use footwork metaphors to talk about faith. The popular poem *Footprints* portrays an image of our walking closely with God and His response when we are unable to walk. Just a few words convey this emotionally powerful idea. Footwork expressions of faith often stand alone without requiring explanation. Consider these common ones:

- walking with God
- following in Jesus' footsteps
- walking by faith
- walking the Christian walk
- learning to walk in ways that please God

These expressions summarize our precious and sometimes precarious faith. The risk is that these words have lost their meaning, that we dismiss them as clichés.

The rich resource of biblical footwork metaphors describe and build an authentic, "on the ground" faith. All scripture comes from the breath of God, preparing and training us (2 Timothy 3:16, 17). The occurrence of hundreds of footwork metaphors in the Bible is a clear sign to pay special attention to our feet.

Right from the opening chapters in Genesis, feet literally and metaphorically make an appearance. They figure into the eternal conflict between good and evil. The enemy nips at our heels as part of the curse of sin: God said, "I will put enmity between you and the woman, and between your offspring and hers; he will crush your head, and you will strike his heel" (Genesis 3:15, NIV).

Follow the trail and listen closely. Footsteps echo throughout the Bible – over land, through and on water, on life-changing roads, and most importantly, into the hearts of believers. From a God who "traces" all our footprints (Job 13:27, NLT) we hear a message of intimacy, overcoming power and heavenly purpose.

Depictions of feet teach us about

- God's holiness: *"Bow low before his feet, for he is holy"* (Psalm 99:5, NLT).
- God's trustworthiness: *"He set my feet on a rock and gave me a firm place to stand"* (Psalm 40:2, NIV).
- The temptations of sin: *"Their feet run to evil"* (Isaiah 59:7, NKJV).
- Powerful promises: *"The God of peace will crush Satan under your feet shortly"* (Romans 16:20, NKJV).

Walking with God provides an array of footwork metaphors that link how we describe and how we live out our faith. By engaging God through the study of these metaphors, this book provides a "jumping off place" into deeper faith.

Introduction

Biblical metaphors have long been a source of spiritual contemplation. The thirteenth-century theologian Thomas Aquinas understood metaphors as one of God's favored ways of communicating. Aquinas, a Dominican priest, believed that God could "write" to us with the physical things He created. God also designed us with the imagination to "read" His message. Common biblical metaphors – such as sheep, rain, and feet – are visible realities whose characteristics reliably teach us about unseen spiritual realities. The tools that God built into creation enable us to discover more about Him and His ways. As my pastor, Andrew Gordon, once said, "God doesn't give us rules for life; He gives us metaphors."

Footwork metaphors are a valuable, yet seldom explored gift from God. This book helps you rediscover and use this gift for a lasting effect on daily spiritual life.

The devotions

Walking with God introduces fifty footwork metaphors for reflection, study, and prayer. Each devotion focuses on a footwork theme that illuminates an understanding of walking with God and an opportunity to coordinate your faith with your feet. Beginning with an invitation, you will discover God's love, presence, strength, touch, leadership, protection, power and purpose as you walk with Him. In the final section you will experience how integral God is to your daily footwork.

The route

The devotions begin with a simple statement of how that footwork metaphor will come to life. Then selected scriptures guide your feet and light your path. (Psalm 119:105) Three movements, Entering, Walking, Following Through, take you back through the verses. They mirror the way you move your feet. They draw their slow, gentle rhythm and their spiritual purpose from the ancient Christian spiritual discipline Lectio Divina, or divine reading. These contemplative movements resemble an attentive stroll. Lectio Divina involves reading portions of scripture multiple times in the company and presence of God. It entails listening to what He says, as you would with a trusted companion. As you enter, walk and follow the route through, He will speak into your life.

ENTERING

Picture yourself on the "threshold" or at the entryway of a time and space with God, ready to engage a particular footwork metaphor literally and figuratively. Entering is an introduction to the metaphor. It may prompt a memory or help thoughts form for a conversation with God later in the chapter. Entering is about preparing for your time of prayer and reflection. During this stage of the route, you pray for God's direction before you start walking with Him through the scripture readings.

WALKING

As you walk through – read through – the passages of scripture, the Holy Spirit will address and bless you. In this stage of the route, you prayerfully engage with the scripture readings and listen for God to speak into your life. To help you in your meditations, you will do different exercises, some creative, some reflective. Jotting down notes makes the experience of this inner walk memorable. Your goal is to listen to your heart and to submit to God's work in you. Don't rush the process – this is not a sprint.

FOLLOWING THROUGH

The important lessons in life are the ones you learn and want to use as soon as possible. After Entering and Walking through the scripture portions, the Following Through part presents an action-oriented opportunity to apply the footwork metaphor to your life. Sometimes, it will help you remember to do or say something or even take on a new "way of walking with God." Other times, it will be about acknowledging a change that has already occurred in you as you moved through the reflection.

As you walk with God, He gently prods you to change and emulate the footwork of Jesus. In Following Through, God looks for your cooperation.

The road ahead

Glance through the table of contents to get a sense of each section and the various footwork metaphors in the Bible. Each metaphor describes choices that God presents in your life; each part of this book encourages you to respond to those choices in faith. Your responses have eternal consequences.

Each chapter follows the same route yet offers a different experience. The introductions bid you onto the path of Bible verses in various translations. Then you engage God as you enter, walk and following through. Each phase involves reflection, prayer, and ultimately an invitation to spiritual growth. How do I know spiritual growth will result? Simply because any encounter with the living God changes you, even if the change is infinitesimal. As writer Anne Lamott has said, "God loves you exactly the way you are, and God loves you too much to let you stay exactly the way you are."

As a reader, you can use *Walking with God* as a personal devotional and source for leisurely contemplation. It can also be a Bible study, with exercises to explore the scriptures, or a resource for spiritual friendships or accountability groups.

The simple purpose of this book is to help you to walk with God with your heart, mind, body, and soul engaged. Surrendering your heart and your feet to God is a step toward understanding what it means to "live and move and have our being" in Him (Acts 17:28, NKJV).

However you use this book, my prayer is that you will become increasingly aware of God's heavenly purposes for your feet, literally and metaphorically.

I

Invitation to "Follow Me" – *Responding to God's Love*

1

Finding God's Path

In trying to find a way forward in life, you naturally ask others about paths they have traveled. The path metaphor in the Bible depicts a close relationship with God through all of life's circumstances.

Psalm 1:6a (NLT)

For the LORD watches over the path of the godly.

Psalm 16:11 (NIV 1984)

You have made known to me the path of life; you will fill me with joy in your presence, with eternal pleasures at your right hand.

Psalm 23:3 (NIV)

He refreshes my soul. He guides me along the right paths for his name's sake.

Psalm 25:4 (NKJV)

Show me Your ways, O LORD; teach me Your paths.

Psalm 119:32 (NIV 1984)

I run in the path of your commands, for you have set my heart free.

Psalm 119:105 (NIV 1984)

Your word is a lamp to my feet and a light for my path.

Proverbs 2:8, 9 (NIV 1984)

For he guards the course of the just and protects the way of his faithful ones. Then you will understand what is right and just and fair—every good path.

Proverbs 3:6 (NLT)

Seek his will in all you do, and he will show you which path to take.

Proverbs 4:11 (NLT)

I will teach you wisdom's ways and lead you in straight paths.

Proverbs 4:26 (NLT)

Mark out a straight path for your feet; stay on the safe path.

Proverbs 12:28 (NIV)

In the way of righteousness there is life; along that path is immortality.

Proverbs 15:19b (NLT)

The path of the upright is an open highway.

ENTERING: Leave the crowd

Options abound for those seeking a spiritual path. Some people would steer you to the notion that all paths lead to God. Or that spiritual enlightenment comes when you overcome the rigors of a difficult path. Jesus' statement *"I am the way, the truth and the life"* reveals the true path to God.

Matthew 7:13, 14 (MSG) says, *"Don't look for shortcuts to God. The market is flooded with surefire, easygoing formulas for a successful life that can be practiced in your spare time. Don't fall for that stuff, even though crowds of people do. The way to life—to God!—is vigorous and requires total attention."*

When you seek God you need a quiet place to listen to His call and His direction. Leave the crowded marketplace where hucksters sell alternative paths as routes to truth. Be still and alone in the presence of God. The Bible offers advice on how to begin: in Matthew 7:7, 8 (NIV 1984), *Jesus says "Ask and it will be given to you; seek and you will find; knock and the door will be opened to you. For everyone who asks receives; he who seeks finds; and to him who knocks, the door will be opened."* The threshold of the path to God is marked with a promise.

A path sets out a route for our feet to follow. Why do you think "path" is such a popular metaphor for spiritual life? Where would you say you are on the path to God?

WALKING: Find the path

Before walking through this devotion, ask the Holy Spirit to show you what you need to see and hear about the path to God. If you are seeking a path or want to be sure about the one you are on, you need discernment. Rely on God to show you the way, at the right pace, through these verses.

On your first reading, find and underline the words that describe God's path. Which ones resonate with what you want for your life? Which ones make you hesitate? Why?

Read the verses a second time. Do you hear the Holy Spirit directing you in some way? If a verse stands out, this is a "sign" to follow. Taken as a whole, your underlined phrases outline God's path. At the top of separate pieces of paper, write the underlined portions. For example:

- path of the godly
- path of life
- right paths
- path of your commands

And so on…

In this exercise, you will use the other words from the verse to illuminate or add light for each description of God's path. If you feel inclined, draw what you see in shapes and colors. These instructions will help you paint your picture in words:

1. Using the words from the verse, find what you think God does.
2. Using the words from the verse, find what God wants you to do.
3. Say each verse aloud and imagine what your feet are doing. Make a note of this footwork on each page.

As you reread the descriptions you have written, ask the Holy Spirit again to show you everything you need to see and hear about the path to God. Ask Him for discernment so that you can say where you are on the path to God. Write a sentence or two about that.

On your final reading, turn these verses into prayers. Use the actual words given from the verses. Psalm 23 offers refreshment, so ask Him to guide you along right paths for His name's sake.

FOLLOWING THROUGH: Follow the signs

Imagine that a friend has asked you for directions in finding the right path. She is confused about the way to go in life, but she is a God-seeker. You may have noted a particular verse that is like a "sign" to you. Everyone is different; verses resonate in each one's inner spirits in unique ways. But perhaps you can help your friend find the sign from Scripture that helps her find the path to God.

From these verses, create some signs that can advise your friend. They might read like this:

- Take the right path.
- Ask God to show you.
- Follow His light.

Review this list of signs. Ask God if you need to listen to this advice.

2

Following Jesus

When Jesus called the disciples, they got up on their feet and left their jobs; they literally followed Him. They soon learned that following was a synchronized motion of heart and feet.

Matthew 4:18, 19 (NIV)

As Jesus was walking beside the Sea of Galilee, he saw two brothers, Simon called Peter and his brother Andrew. They were casting a net into the lake, for they were fishermen. "Come, follow me," Jesus said, "and I will send you out to fish for people."

Matthew 8:19–22 (NIV)

Then a teacher of the law came to him and said, "Teacher, I will follow you wherever you go." Jesus replied, "Foxes have dens and birds have nests, but the Son of Man has no place to lay his head." Another disciple said to him, "Lord, first let me go and bury my father." But Jesus told him, "Follow me, and let the dead bury their own dead."

Matthew 16:24, 25 (NIV)

Then Jesus said to his disciples, "Whoever wants to be my disciple must deny themselves and take up their cross and follow me. For whoever wants to save their life will lose it, but whoever loses their life for me will find it."

Matthew 19:27–30 (NLT)

Then Peter said to him, "We've given up everything to follow you. What will we get?" Jesus replied, "I assure you that when the world is made new and the Son of Man sits upon his glorious throne, you who have been my followers will also sit on twelve thrones, judging the twelve tribes of Israel. And everyone who has given up houses or brothers or sisters or father or mother or children or property, for my sake, will receive a hundred times as much in return and will inherit eternal life. But many who are the greatest now will be least important then, and those who seem least important now will be the greatest then."

ENTERING: Accounting for the metaphor

When Jesus invited His first disciples to join God's Kingdom, He said they would "fish for people." As fishermen, they responded to that. The metaphor Jesus used gave them a picture of their role in His Kingdom. This simple occupational metaphor contained an amazing vision. From a twenty-first-century perspective, you might understand "fishing for people" as evangelism.

Now, if the disciples had had different professions or passions, would Jesus have altered what He said? The fishing metaphor spoke to them, and it can also speak to you. Our Creator knows how to inspire you. Imagine the metaphors that could tap into the breadth of vocational purposes. What if, on the road that day, Jesus had invited artists, accountants, airline pilots, architects, army officers, acrobats, or animators? Imagine the variety of Kingdom metaphors!

How would Jesus call you to your Kingdom purpose?

WALKING: Calculating the costs

Continuing on the same track of professions and purposes, walk through these verses as an accountant, pen and paper in hand. Let the Holy Spirit audit your responses.

On your first reading, notice how idealistic enthusiasm to follow Jesus meets the reality of family and political pressure. Jesus warns His followers, and He doesn't mince words. He insists that they assess the cost of following Him. Amazingly and thankfully, He also describes benefits above and beyond what they had ever hoped for.

In this devotion, you will survey the costs and their implications of following Jesus. Ask the Holy Spirit to help you verify which costs are difficult to understand or to manage on your own:

- There is no place to lay your head.
    - The future may be unpredictable or uncomfortable.
- Deny yourself.
    - Yield all personal priorities to Jesus.
    - Let go of self-absorption.
- Take up your cross.
    - Remember what Jesus achieved on the cross for you.
- Give up everything.
    - Don't let anything compete with your heart's attention.
- Don't try to save your life or avoid any difficulties in it.
    - Resist trying to fix things on your own.

Do you sense God is preparing you to face one of those costs?

FOLLOWING THROUGH: Getting to the bottom line

It's hard to follow Jesus. There's opposition to and competition for the attention of your heart. There are roadblocks; there are some who think of you as a laughingstock. It can get very taxing. (Okay, no more accounting terms!)

Even the disciples deserted Jesus for a time, backing away under pressure (Matthew 26:56). You can fall off for a season and He brings you back. Sound familiar? As important as obedience is, following isn't about how strong or capable you are. Jesus' disciples were cowering when He breathed the Holy Spirit into them after His death and resurrection (John 20:22). And they were hiding (albeit waiting) after His ascension, when the Holy Spirit dramatically descended on them (Acts 2). Jesus equipped them to faithfully withstand the pressures, even unto death.

He will do the same for you. Ask Him.

3

Running the Race

For St. Paul, running the race is a metaphor for life: starting, staying in, finishing, and winning. He is not a lone runner; he has a role for you on his team.

Acts 20:24 (NIV 1984)

I consider my life worth nothing to me, if only I may finish the race and complete the task the LORD Jesus has given me—the task of testifying to the gospel of God's grace.

1 Corinthians 9:24–27 (NIV 1984)

Do you not know that in a race all the runners run, but only one gets the prize? Run in such a way as to get the prize. Everyone who competes in the games goes into strict training. They do it to get a crown that will not last; but we do it to get a crown that will last forever. Therefore I do not run like a man running aimlessly; I do not fight like a man beating the air. No, I beat my body and make it my slave so that after I have preached to others, I myself will not be disqualified for the prize.

Galatians 2:2 (NLT)

I went there because God revealed to me that I should go. While I was there I met privately with those considered to be leaders of the church and shared with them the message I had been preaching to the Gentiles. I wanted to make sure that we were in agreement, for fear that all my efforts had been wasted and I was running the race for nothing.

Galatians 5:7, 8 (MSG)

You were running superbly! Who cut in on you, deflecting you from the true course of obedience? This detour doesn't come from the One who called you into the race in the first place.

Philippians 2:16 (NLT)

Hold firmly to the word of life; then, on the day of Christ's return, I will be proud that I did not run the race in vain and that my work was not useless.

Philippians 3:12 (MSG)

I'm not saying that I have this all together, that I have it made. But I am well on my way, reaching out for Christ, who has so wondrously reached out for me. Friends, don't get me wrong: By no means do I count myself an expert in all of this, but I've got my eye on the goal, where God is beckoning us onward—to Jesus. I'm off and running and I'm not turning back.

Hebrews 12:1, 2 (NLT)

Therefore, since we are surrounded by such a huge crowd of witnesses to the life of faith, let us strip off every weight that slows us down, especially the sin that so easily trips us up. And let us run with endurance the race God has set before us. We do this by keeping our eyes on Jesus, the champion who initiates and perfects our faith. Because of the joy awaiting him, he endured the cross, disregarding its shame. Now he is seated in the place of honor beside God's throne.

2 Timothy 4:6–8 (MSG)

You take over. I'm about to die, my life an offering on God's altar. This is the only race worth running. I've run hard right to the finish, believed all the way. All that's left now is the shouting—God's applause! Depend on it, he's an honest judge. He'll do right not only by me, but by everyone eager for his coming.

ENTERING: In the starting block

He wants you on his team. In this devotion, St. Paul speaks as a retiring coach. You know his history: once he got on track with Jesus, he was God's marathon messenger. Today, he is checking the fitness of his teammates as they run the race that God has set out for them. Are your running shoes nearby? If you are in this race, your faith and your feet are going to get a workout!

Head down to the track and hear what Paul is saying. You know his voice: relentless in passion and persuasion. There he is, giving a pep talk to the runners. People are scattered over the lawn, tightening their shoe laces and stretching. "The way we run a race is the way we live our lives!" he yells to those doing their warm-up laps. Everyone here was up at the crack of dawn, doing sprints, and training for endurance. He keeps reminding them of the prize, Christ Himself.

Some of the runners do a trial relay as a team-building exercise. Paul shouts from the starting gate, "Hold the baton firmly; reach out to the next runner; let the next one take over." That's the way Christ trained him to move the gospel.

Coach Paul is looking for new recruits. Where do you stand? Are your feet itching to be in the starting block? Or is cheering from the sidelines close enough for you? Today he wants prospective team members, with little or no experience, to see the runners in action. Paul will walk through these passages with you. No running. Not yet. You need to get a sense of the course and what kind of training is involved.

He wants you on his team. He speaks for Jesus when he says that.

WALKING: From strength to strength

Runners pass by as you walk along the track and listen to Paul. Read all the verses through once. In it, he summarizes his experience. He also calls out to one of the runners and addresses you as a new recruit. He is clearly serious: "Life is worth nothing.… I made my body a slave.… I did not run the race in vain." There are more examples. Stop after every verse, and try stepping into Paul's shoes. Could you say the same things about yourself? Take extra time with this. What do you think of Paul's standards?

As you walk along, Coach Paul stretches out his arms to describe the race course. His body language matches the verses; to race is to live. He is so devoted! "Do you know why I run this race?" he asks you.

Go through the verses again to understand why a runner runs. Paul sets out Jesus as His example in the Hebrews verse. Now what do you think about Paul's standards? Dig deeper for Paul's motivation and his goals.

- Why did he get into the race?
- What keeps him in?
- How does he want to finish it?
- Who is watching?

Paul uncharacteristically winks and says, "Here's the shortcut through this passage: Look for Jesus in everything I say and do." So you check every verse. Then he gives you a new-recruit application form and says, "Write down why you want to run the race." So you do. What a taskmaster!

Tomorrow, the "strength to strength" training begins. Apparently, "strip off the weight of sin and then run" is the first event. As Paul turns to leave he says, "Just keep your eyes on Jesus. He is the prize. That's all you have to remember." He heads off at a steady trot. Thanks coach!

FOLLOWING THROUGH: In the relay

Some people run for real; others just run in their imaginations. Running to Jesus as the prize is spiritually real. And isn't running a joy! There is something amazing about having two feet off the ground, even if it is for a millisecond.

As you do your "practice laps of prayer" tonight, ask the Holy Spirit to teach you more about the relay. Remember how Christ trained Paul, "Hold the baton firmly; reach out to the next runner; let the next one take over." In your mind, feel the paperweight of the word of God in your hand; then as you live and move and have your being in Him each day, pass the truth and grace that is in Jesus Christ on to others. Relay complete! Feel the pleasure of your heavenly coach.

When you put on your shoes tomorrow, remember that Paul wants you to be a fellow runner, not a competitor. Pray about that next team-runner that you will pass the gospel to. He or she may be a new recruit.

4

Running with the Message

When you receive a message that is true and life-changing, you probably feel compelled to tell others. Your feet get moving and spreading the message gains momentum.

Habakkuk 2:2 (NLT)

Then the LORD said to me, "Write my answer [revelation] plainly on tablets, so that a runner can carry the correct message to others."

Luke 24:32–35 (MSG)

Back and forth they talked. "Didn't we feel on fire as he conversed with us on the road, as he opened up the Scriptures for us?" They didn't waste a minute. They were up and on their way back to Jerusalem. They found the Eleven and their friends gathered together, talking away: "It's really happened! The Master has been raised up—Simon saw him!"

Then the two went over everything that happened on the road and how they recognized him when he broke the bread.

John 4:28–30, 39–42 (NLT)

The woman left her water jar beside the well and ran back to the village, telling everyone, "Come and see a man who told me everything I ever did! Could he possibly be the Messiah?" So the people came streaming from the village to see him....

Many Samaritans from the village believed in Jesus because the woman had said, "He told me everything I ever did!" When they came out to see him, they begged him to stay in their village. So he stayed for two days, long enough for many more to hear his message and believe. Then they said to the woman, "Now we believe, not just because of what you told us, but because we have heard him ourselves. Now we know that he is indeed the Savior of the world."

Acts 10:36, 44 (NLT)

This is the message of Good News for the people of Israel—that there is peace with God through Jesus Christ, who is LORD of all.... Even as Peter was saying these things, the Holy Spirit fell upon all who were listening to the message.

Acts 17:11 (NIV)

They received the message with great eagerness and examined the Scriptures every day to see if what Paul said was true.

Romans 10:17 (NIV)

Consequently, faith comes from hearing the message, and the message is heard through the word about Christ.

Isaiah 52:7 (NLT)

How beautiful on the mountains are the feet of the messenger who brings good news, the good news of peace and salvation, the news that the God of Israel reigns!

ENTERING: Getting the message

In ancient times, runners carried messages between kingdoms or from commanders to their soldiers. Light-footed movement through treacherous places presents a picture of obedient determination. With hands gripping scrolls, runners were neutral participants. They simply delivered the message, not having written it or knowing what it contained. Our current-day equivalent is UPS or FedEx services, who expedite unseen messages.

The gospel's messengers were a different sort: untrained and passionate, running with a sense of urgency. When they received the message of forgiveness and the resurrected Christ in their hearts, it gripped and compelled them. Relaying it to others was the next natural move. The impact on their hearts led to their feet impacting the ground. The Spirit of God directed them.

How does this picture of hearts and feet in alignment relate to you and your life? Telephone, email, texting, and Skype shrink our distances. Is it more about fingers than feet these days? How can your feet play a role in bringing the message of the living Christ to others? Perhaps, smaller steps are the challenge to you. Would you go out of your way to speak with others? Do you use the opportunity of proximity when standing in line? Do you stop to help strangers in need? Your feet can still bring and even "run with" the gospel message of peace and compassion.

So, how should you connect with the footwork in this devotion? Close your eyes. Picture a passionate runner for Christ relaying His message. Retain this picture. When you contemplate this image and the verses that describe how the Spirit moved people to run with the message, you will receive instruction for your heart.

WALKING: Carrying the message

Some messages compel you to move with lightning speed. When they are timely and personal, they activate your entire being – body, mind, and spirit. On your first reading of the verses, underline all the phrases describing Jesus and His heavenly purposes on earth. Why did the people hearing about Jesus spring into action? Ask the Holy Spirit to write the same message permanently on your heart. Then write the words down, as from God to you, on a separate piece of paper.

On your second reading, stay with the verses that describe people receiving the good news. Picture the interactions. What was passed between them? Was it a story? Close your eyes and think of stories as "batons" passing between runners. Recall your first hearing of and connecting with the story of Jesus on the cross. Who passed this gospel message to you? Did you hear that person describe how the power or love of God had changed his or her life? Have you since retold that story to others, adding your own personal details?

Holding the image of a baton, look at Acts 10. The message of peace with God the Father is passed through God the Son, then on to Peter who, filled with the Holy Spirit, passed it on to others. Relay teams are God's design.

As you read through these selected verses for a final time, pause at the phrase "God's answer" in the first verse. What do you think the question might have been?

FOLLOWING THROUGH: Passing it on

Think back to the message the Holy Spirit imprinted on your heart that you then wrote on paper. Ask God to make it permanent. One way to make it memorable at least, is to speak that message aloud to someone else. Another way is to roll up that piece of paper and tie it with a ribbon. Look for someone who needs to receive it, and then get moving. Move your feet. Pass the baton.

5

Walking in His Ways

The way God wants you to walk is how He defines His character. Would you say the same for yourself?

Psalm 26:2, 3 (NIV 1984)

Test me, O LORD, and try me, examine my heart and my mind; for your love is ever before me, and I walk continually in your truth.

Psalm 119:45 (NLT)

I will walk in freedom, for I have devoted myself to your commandments.

Isaiah 33:15, 16 (NIV 1984)

He who walks righteously and speaks what is right ... this is the man who will dwell on the heights, whose refuge will be the mountain fortress.

Luke 1:76, 79b (ESV)

"And you, child [John the Baptist], will be called the prophet of the Most High; for you will go before the Lord to prepare his ways ... to guide our feet into the way of peace."

Ephesians 2:10 (NKJV)

For, we are His workmanship, created in Christ Jesus for good works, which God prepared beforehand that we should walk in them.

Ephesians 4:1–3 (ESV)

I therefore, a prisoner for the LORD, urge you to walk in a manner worthy of the calling to which you have been called, with all humility and gentleness, with patience, bearing with one another in love, eager to maintain the unity of the Spirit in the bond of peace.

Ephesians 5:1, 2 (ESV)

Therefore be imitators of God, as beloved children. And walk in love, as Christ loved us and gave himself up for us, a fragrant offering and sacrifice to God.

Colossians 1:10 (NKJV)

Walk worthy of the LORD, fully pleasing Him, being fruitful in every good work and increasing in the knowledge of God.

2 John 1:6 (NIV 1984)

And this is love: that we walk in obedience to his commands. As you have heard from the beginning, his command is that you walk in love.

ENTERING: Game plan

If you devised a board game or a card game, you would write the rules down in some orderly fashion. Players would learn how to start the game, how to compete, and how to win. You might play a practice round so that the new initiates got the hang of it.

God designed a game plan to teach people how to walk with Him and with each other. His guidelines, the Ten Commandments, were based on love and mutual respect. He wrote them on tablets of stone and gave them to Moses. In no time at all, God's people, newly initiated to the rules, started breaking them. God didn't throw out the rules, but He changed His strategy. He revised the game plan: He would literally walk with His people, model how to walk in His ways, and make a way for all players to win.

In God's new plan, grace was the strategy: "*It is by grace that you have been saved*" (Ephesians 2:5, NIV 1984). He sent in His Son to show how to play the game: walk obediently with God and walk compassionately with others. Jesus was the "game demo" of how to walk in God's ways. He was the walking rule book – a walking testimony of grace. He made a way for all the ruler-breakers to win when He temporarily folded His hand, stood in for them, and took their losses. But He came back to show them that winning was His plan for them all along.

It may surprise you to discover how absolutely gracious God is. As you pray through this devotion, ask God for a new understanding of His ways so that He can rule in your heart.

WALKING: Grace plan

Ask Jesus to keep you close company as you walk and stop at different places in these scriptures.

Let Psalm 26:2 be the game opener: ask God to help you examine your heart. Stay in that place until He moves you along. When ready, consciously walk with His love before you and constantly ask Him to show you His truth as you go along.

First, highlight the phrases that describe walking in God's ways. Each one is a high ideal and is what Jesus has already achieved for you. For example: walking in good works, walking with all humility and walking in love. Don't they seem more like attributes or attitudes? Imagine the way your feet would move, as you contemplate each verse. What does walking in freedom look like in your life? What would be the way of peace with your neighbors?

On second reading, go slowly. At each verse, ask Jesus a question about how He walked that way on earth. Choose one or two verses and then meditate on His life, His death, and His resurrection. For example, Psalm 119 refers to "walking in freedom" and "devotion to God's commandments." Think about the different times that Jesus was criticized by the Pharisees for "breaking the rules." Did He actually break God's commandments or man-made rules? How did He demonstrate walking in freedom? The Gospels make many references to physical and spiritual healing that Jesus freely gave in many of those critical encounters. Contemplate this verse and others, asking Jesus to show you how walking in God's ways empowers you to do His will.

Finally, ask God for more grace for the day. Ask Him to mobilize you in His game plan for your life.

FOLLOWING THROUGH: Follow-up plan

The figurative expression "walking in His ways" describes the way you move – in close and in casual relationships. It characterizes your heart and what others see in you. They may not know what they sense about you, but it draws them to you. Ideally, they would see Jesus as you walk and would want to follow Him, too.

Is there one attribute that you think others might actually see in you? Return to the phrases you highlighted. Is there another one that you long for? Ask Jesus to show you how to walk that way. Underline it. Memorize it. Write it on a small piece of paper and put it in your shoe.

II

Transformation in One Step - *Pivoting to God's Presence*

6

Arise!

The motion of rising on your feet in response to God's command is a picture of resurrection. In scripture, rising up is a sign that God has something new under way. In these passages I have added emphasis on the pertinent terms.

Matthew 2:13a (NIV 1984)

When they had gone, an angel of the LORD appeared to Joseph in a dream. "<u>Get up</u>," he said, "take the child and his mother and escape to Egypt."

Matthew 17:5–7 (NIV 1984)

While he was still speaking, a bright cloud enveloped them, and a voice from the cloud said, "This is my Son, whom I love; with him I am well pleased. Listen to him!" When the disciples heard this, they fell facedown to the ground, terrified. But Jesus came and touched them. "<u>Get up</u>," he said. "Don't be afraid."

Matthew 28:6 (NKJV)

He is not here; for He <u>is risen</u>, as He said. Come, see the place where the Lord lay.

Luke 5:23 (NKJV)

"Which is easier, to say, 'Your sins are forgiven you,' or to say, 'Rise up and walk'?"

Luke 8:52b–55a (NIV 1984)

"Stop wailing," Jesus said. "She is not dead but asleep." They laughed at him, knowing that she was dead. But he took her by the hand and said, "My child, get up!" Her spirit returned, and at once she stood up.

Luke 22:46 (NIV 1984)

"Why are you sleeping?" he asked them. "Get up and pray so that you will not fall into temptation."

Acts 3:6 (NKJV)

Then Peter said, "Silver and gold I do not have, but what I do have I give you: In the name of Jesus Christ of Nazareth, rise up and walk."

Acts 26:16 (NIV 1984)

(To Saul on the road to Damascus) *"Now get up and stand on your feet. I have appeared to you to appoint you as a servant and as a witness of what you have seen of me and what I will show you."*

Revelation 11:11 (AMP)

But after three and a half days, by God's gift the breath of life again entered into them, and they rose up on their feet, and great dread and terror fell on those who watched them.

ENTERING: Reading the signs

The greatest marvel of Jesus' life was His death and resurrection. Jesus told His mystified disciples that He would rise again in three days. (See Mark 8:31; 9:9, 31; 10:34.) He also referred more obliquely to the sign of Jonah (Matthew 16:4) in a conversation with the well-schooled Pharisees. Despite these advance warnings, His resurrection still stunned His followers. It revolutionized their thinking; Jesus had overcome death. Christians commemorate the significance of Jesus' resurrection each Easter, saying "He is risen" and responding "He is risen, indeed."

Resurrection in daily life follows the pattern of Jesus' obedience to God the Father: to "die to self" and "rise to life." By Christ's example, you learn to submit to God's work in you and trust your Heavenly Father for whatever change is to come. It is daunting until you get to know the grace-filled touch of God.

This devotion offers examples of people rising at God's behest, becoming evidence of resurrection in daily life. Listen for the Holy Spirit's bidding you to rise, to get up. This is His encouragement to you. Soon you will see that God has something fresh and new under way for you.

WALKING: Living the resurrection

On your first reading, go slowly. Put yourself in each scene and focus on the footwork. Notice the ordinary actions, such as getting out of bed, and the extraordinary or supernatural actions, such as rising from the dead. What does the footwork symbolize to you?

As you reread, sense the suddenness and surprise in each situation. If you are not familiar with the ongoing story that verses are excerpted from, go to the Bible and read the chapter. Use the margin beside each verse to note what God is doing in that situation. For example, In Matthew 2, God wants them to leave the country so that Jesus isn't killed by King Herod. What does it take for each person to get up on his feet and respond to what God is doing? Courage? Faith? Obedience? Trust? Or something else?

Think for a moment about the pattern of resurrection: dying to self and rising to life. Go through each verse again and imagine what the people involved would have had to "die to." Look for grief, despair, disease, hopes and plans, fear, esteem or lack of it, and so on. Do any of these resemble the challenges in your own life?

Finally, go back through each verse and imagine what new thing or change in life God wanted to give the people involved. Look for physical mobility, faith and conviction, comfort in God's presence, salvation, anointing for ministry, and more. Which of these attracts you? Form a prayer in your heart asking God to surprise you with your heart's desire for change.

FOLLOWING THROUGH: Rejecting the status quo

The life in Christ is a life of change, whether you call it redemption or sanctification or being conformed to the likeness of Christ. Have you heard the expression, "God loves you too much to leave you that way?" Reflect on what you would like to change, and recognize that you need God to do it. Allow the desire for change to surface, and prepare your heart to listen to and obey God's Spirit.

God wants you to live the resurrection. He wants you to rise up.

7

Returning to God

You may be watching and waiting for a wayward child to return home, for the sound of familiar footsteps approaching. The parable of the prodigal son helps you listen to God's emphatic promises to the one returning.

Chronicles 30:9b (NIV 1984)

The LORD your God is gracious and compassionate. He will not turn his face from you if you return to him.

Job 22:23a (NIV 1984)

If you return to the Almighty, you will be restored.

Isaiah 30:15b (NLT)

Only in returning to me and resting in me will you be saved. In quietness and confidence is your strength.

Isaiah 44:22b (NLT)

Oh, return to me, for I have paid the price to set you free.

Jeremiah 15:19 (NLT)

If you return to me, I will restore you so you can continue to serve me.

Lamentations 3:40 (NIV 1984)

Let us examine our ways and test them, and let us return to the LORD.

Hosea 14:1, 2, 4 (NLT)

Return, O Israel, to the Lord your God, for your sins have brought you down. Bring your confessions, and return to the Lord. Say to him, "Forgive all our sins and graciously receive us, so that we may offer you our praises."...

The Lord says, "Then I will heal you of your faithlessness; my love will know no bounds, for my anger will be gone forever."

Malachi 3:7b (NIV 1984)

Return to me and I will return to you.

ENTERING: Missing the prodigals

In public buildings such as malls, sports centers, and schools, there is usually a lost-and-found box under a service counter. Rightful owners go there to look for their missing possessions. The Kingdom of God is like this. Jesus taught about the restoration of the lost and damaged prodigal son who returned home to his ever-hopeful father (Luke 15:11–32).

The prodigal son story may trigger two responses in you. First, it may renew your eagerness to see your own wayward child come home. As a parent, you understand the agony of the wait and you anticipate the joy of the welcome. Also, you may be able to retrace your own path home to God. Your experiences were a 180, a complete turnaround of heart and feet. Did you wonder how God would receive you? That's what your child is probably wondering too. In the parable of the prodigal, Jesus teaches you who God is and He teaches you how to be – whether the parent or the child. He told the parable to reassure you: God is always listening for approaching steps and is ready to meet the prodigal en route. His way of receiving the wayward child is your model for how to do likewise.

If you are losing strength as you endure the wait of a loved one's return, this devotion will remind you of God's character and His promise of reconciliation. Pray in advance that His words will help you focus all your expectations on Him. Release the work of return fully to the Lord God Almighty. Full-throttle release.

WALKING: Embracing the prodigals

Read the all the verses aloud in the voice of a father calling out to a lost child. Listen from the child's point of view. What do you hear? Underline the words that touch your heart.

Now, contemplate God's promises. Were these the words that you underlined? Do they stir your heart to faith, remembering how God received you when you returned to Him? Ask the Holy Spirit to extend that faith for the return of your lost loved one.

On your second reading, notice that there are three voices in these scriptures:

- God's
- those recommending God
- the prodigals'

In the margin, make a note of the different speakers. In the Hosea verse, all three are speaking. Using all the verses, create a dialogue among all three voices. Which verse do you begin with and end with?

Finally, say each verse aloud with thanksgiving because Jesus found you when you were lost, and His work on the cross made a way home to the Father for you and your loved ones.

FOLLOWING THROUGH: Releasing the prodigals

God's timing for a return may not coincide with your sense of time management. His is always perfect; it has purpose. He knows the changes He wants to make in wayward hearts before they return. He always asks you to trust Him. God loves your lost loved ones and wants the return as much or more than you do. So, release them to your Heavenly Father, who is more capable and compassionate than anyone.

Use these verses to begin a prayer for your lost one. Adjust the words:

- using your loved one's name
- saying not "if" but "when"
- emphasizing the promises because God will keep them

After you have prayed, wait – as on the road of return – anticipating what God will do. Think positively, in belief, with full-on trust. Begin to plan the celebration.

8

Turning to God

Toe to toe and face to face with God is where He wants to be with you. Check your feet and consider turning to Him from where you are right now.

Deuteronomy 30:10 (NLT)

The LORD your God will delight in you if you obey his voice and keep the commands and decrees written in this Book of Instruction, and if you turn to the LORD your God with all your heart and soul.

1 Kings 8:58 (NIV 1984)

May he turn our hearts to him, to walk in all his ways and to keep the commands, decrees and regulations he gave our fathers.

Psalm 119:36 (NIV 1984)

Turn my heart toward your statutes and not toward selfish gain.

Psalm 119:59 (NIV 1984)

I have considered my ways and have turned my steps to your statutes.

Isaiah 45:22 (NIV 1984)

"Turn to me and be saved, all you ends of the earth; for I am God, and there is no other."

Isaiah 55:6, 7 (NLT)

Seek the LORD while you can find him. Call on him now while he is near. Let the wicked change their ways and banish every thought of doing wrong. Let them turn to the LORD that he may have mercy on them. Yes, turn to our God, for he will forgive generously.

Mark 4:12 (NLT)

"'They will turn to me and be forgiven.'"

Acts 3:19 (NIV 1984)

Repent, then, and turn to God, so that your sins may be wiped out, that times of refreshing may come from the Lord.

ENTERING: Attention deficit

A grandmother recounted a story of caring for her ten-year-old grandson. She described an over-active, unruly boy who always crashed into things. She loved her busy grandson even if he rarely listened to her. One day she took his precious precocious face into her soft hands and held his face gently in front of her own. She had his attention, finally.

This presents a picture of God's yearning to hold you and you not holding still. You may be a restless, preoccupied person. Your to-do lists are long. Distractible is your middle name. God patiently takes your face in His hands to get your attention. Almighty God wants your eyes on Him.

Where are you on the scale of 1–10 in distractibility? Have you taken time lately to listen to God? Are you the "Martha of many plans" in the kitchen or the "Mary of much devotion" at the feet of Jesus? (Luke 10:38–42)

As you prepare to enter the time of devotion, what do you expect to hear in your heart? What does "turning to God" mean to you? Is any part of you resisting?

Get ready to pivot to God. He is waiting.

WALKING: Rules for the unruly

Read the verses several times. What caught your attention? Did anything surprise or confuse you? Turn to your Heavenly Father, full face, and confess any contrary feelings about commands, decrees from on high, regulations, or statutes of law. Rebellious children are His specialty.

Read through the scriptures again and listen to God express Himself as you begin the motion of turning to Him. Listen for joy and generosity, rest and restoration beckoning you. He extends forgiveness and reconciliation to get you back on track with Him.

God knows what holds your attention. Reread Deuteronomy 30:10 and underline what gets His attention. He is a God of order and consistency. In His passionate love for you, He makes promises with an eternal warranty. Even though He designed you to be obedient, rules are not His favorite way to corral you. Loving pursuit is more His style. His hope is that you will respond to that love and turn to Him. But you are in a distractible, disobedient generation – no different than previous ones. So His rules are like His hands on your face. They help you pay attention.

Imagine God with His hands on your face right now. He is gently turning you and your life toward Him. Reread Mark 4, and receive a gift that will lighten your next step.

FOLLOWING THROUGH: Attention intact

Spend some time with the chorus from this song. Read or sing it a few times. Let the Holy Spirit show you what is "growing dim." Ask Jesus to hold your face in His hands as He gently turns you, heart and feet, onto His path for tomorrow.

> "Turn your eyes upon Jesus. Look full in His wonderful face,
> And the things of earth will grow strangely dim,
> In the light of His glory and grace".

As we close, make a list of all the things you need to do today. Did something happen inside you as you went through this devotion that now makes creating this list a chore? Good move!

9

Walking from Darkness to Light

Just as your physical senses attune to changes in the environment, your ears and eyes adjust as you approach God's presence. Metaphors of light and dark direct your footwork in this spiritual experience.

Psalm 18:28b (NIV)

My God turns my darkness into light.

Psalm 23:4 (NLT)

Even when I walk through the darkest valley, I will not be afraid, for you are close beside me.

Psalm 56:13b (NLT)

So now I can walk in Your presence, O God, in your life-giving light.

Psalm 89:15 (NLT)

Happy are those who hear the joyful call to worship, for they will walk in the light of your presence, Lord.

Isaiah 9:1, 2 (NLT)

*Nevertheless that time of darkness and despair will not go on forever....
There will be a time ... filled with glory. The people who walk in darkness
will see a great light. For those who live in a land of deep darkness, a light
will shine.*

Isaiah 50:10b (NLT)

*If you are walking in darkness, without a ray of light, trust in the LORD
and rely on your God.*

Isaiah 58:9b, 10 (NIV 1984)

*If you do away with the yoke of oppression, with the pointing finger and
malicious talk, and if you spend yourselves in behalf of the hungry and
satisfy the needs of the oppressed, then your light will rise in the darkness,
and your night will become like the noonday.*

Ephesians 5:8 (NKJV)

*For you were once in darkness, but now you are light in the Lord. Walk
as children of light.*

1 Peter 2:9 (NIV 1984)

*But you are a chosen people, a royal priesthood, a holy nation, a people
belonging to God, that you may declare the praises of him who called you
out of darkness into his wonderful light.*

1 John 1:6, 7 (NKJV)

*If we say that we have fellowship with Him, and walk in darkness, we lie
and do not practice the truth. But if we walk in the light as He is in the*

light, we have fellowship with one another, and the blood of Jesus Christ His Son cleanses us from all sin.

ENTERING: Adjusting to the light

You know how your eyes react when you leave a dark room and enter a brightly lit one. Matinee movie-goers feel this brief blindness as they exit. So too, when you walk out of spiritual darkness, your eyes need to adjust to the light. You forget, even after a spiritual matinee in the dark, that God is welcoming and trustworthy. He hasn't changed, but you have. Darkness can permeate your heart and block you from hearing or seeing well, spiritually speaking. Your re-entry into God's light might be on flimsy faith. Hesitant steps follow a compelling voice. You start tuning out the competing, badgering voices. Hearing Him builds your trust with each step into His light, His presence.

The key to moving from the darkness to light is in listening for and distinguishing God's voice. God speaks in recognizable ways in the Bible:

- He makes simple declarations: "I AM" is the name that He gave for Himself to Moses (Exodus 3:14).
- He commands His people: "Follow me" is how Jesus' disciples began their walk with Him.
- He makes conditional commitments because He is looking for cooperative partners: "If my people, who are called by my name, will humble themselves and pray and seek my face and turn from their wicked ways, then will I hear from heaven and will forgive their sin and will heal their land (2 Chronicles 7:14, NIV 1984).
- He also makes unconditional promises: "I will be with you" (Exodus 3:12, NIV 1984).

Ask the Holy Spirit to help you get ready to walk from darkness to light. Lean on God. Listen with your ears and your heart.

WALKING: Responding to the light

As you read through the scriptures for the first time, which verse gets your attention? Rest awhile and repeat that verse, emphasizing different words. While recognizing God's voice is key to moving out of the darkness, responding to Him is essential to staying in the light.

Go back through all the verses now and notice the patterns of

- declarations
- commands
- conditional commitments
- unconditional promises

King David thunders a declaration about God in Psalm 18. Are you surprised by God's power to change your life? There are several more declarations. Each one starts with "you are." What does God say about you? Make a list, personalizing it with "I am…"

When you think of the word "command," what comes to mind? There are commands in these verses. Do you think that they are typical commands? What do they tell you about the person issuing them? How do you respond to them and to Him? Think of your response as obedience.

God makes commitments that require your participation. Circle every "if." One part of the sentence depends on the other. With a little license taken, here is an example: "Even when [if] I walk through the darkest valley, I will not be afraid, for you are close beside me." God wants you to trust Him in your low emotions and lousy circumstances. If you can do that, you have the assurance of His presence. What does He want from you in Isaiah 58? Does this suggest a path for you to follow? And, what about the verse in 1 John? God doesn't want you to be fooled into thinking you're walking in the light when really, you're skirting the shadows. Is this getting personal?

Finally, God makes some beautiful promises as you walk from darkness to light. Underline and try to memorize every phrase that uses the word "will." This word signals promise; it points directly to God's will.

FOLLOWING THROUGH: Staying in the light

Your senses are newly awake. First, your ears are alert to the call. Then, your eyes see clarity, depth, motion, and color. Your body responds, obediently taking in the light of Christ. Darkness and its voices abate.

Try this symbolic act: spend some time alone in a darkened room. Acknowledge things that have separated you from God. Listen for His voice prompting you to leave the room. Enter the light with thanksgiving. Then, ask God to fill you with the light of Christ.

III

Coordination of Faith and Feet
– *Experiencing God's Strength*

10

Heart and Soles

Piano students often learn to play the duet called Heart and Soul as an early experience of coordinating with another player. Accompaniment is a musical metaphor of how God coordinates His heart with yours. "Heart and Soles" is word play revealing how God orchestrates your walk with Him.

Prelude:

Psalm 139:23, 24 (NLT)

(Chorus) *Search me, O God, and know my heart; test me and know my anxious thoughts. Point out anything in me that offends you, and lead me along the path of everlasting life.*

First Movement:

Deuteronomy 28:65 (NIV 1984)

Among those nations you will find no repose, no resting place for the sole of your foot. There the LORD will give you an anxious mind, eyes weary with longing, and a despairing heart.

1 Kings 8:23 (NKJV)

(Chorus) *"LORD God of Israel, there is no God in heaven above or on earth below like You, who keep Your covenant and mercy with Your servants who walk before You with all their hearts."*

1 Kings 8:57a, 58a (NKJV)

(Chorus) *May the LORD our God ... incline our hearts to Himself, to walk in all His ways.*

Second Movement:

Isaiah 3:16 (NIV 1984)

The LORD says, "The women of Zion are haughty, walking along with outstretched necks, flirting with their eyes, tripping along with mincing steps, with ornaments jingling on their ankles."

Proverbs 6:18 (NIV 1984)

[I detest] A heart that devises wicked schemes, feet that are quick to rush into evil.

Proverbs 7:11 (NKJV)

She was loud and rebellious, Her feet would not stay at home.

Psalm 143:8b (NLT)

(Chorus) *Show me where to walk, for I give myself to you.*

Isaiah 38:3a (NIV 1984)

(Chorus) *"Remember, O LORD, how I have walked before you faithfully and with wholehearted devotion and have done what is good in your eyes."*

Third Movement:

Ezekiel 11:19, 20 (ESV)

And I will give them one heart, and a new spirit I will put within them. I will remove the heart of stone from their flesh and give them a heart of flesh, that they may walk in my statutes and keep my rules and obey them. And they shall be my people, and I will be their God.

Jeremiah 31:13a (NLT)

The young women will dance for joy, and the men—old and young—will join in the celebration. I will turn their mourning into joy.

2 Samuel 6:14 (NLT)

(Chorus) *And David danced before the LORD with all his might.*

Postlude:

Psalm 139:1–5 (NLT)

(Chorus) *O LORD, you have examined my heart and know everything about me. You know when I sit down or stand up. You know my thoughts even when I'm far away. You see me when I travel and when I rest at home. You know everything I do. You know what I am going to say even before I say it, LORD. You go before me and follow me. You place your hand of blessing on my head.*

ENTERING: Knowing the score

After September 11, 2001 Nick Peros, a Canadian classical composer, used scripture to create a dialogue between God and humanity. The voices of Father, Son, and Spirit in the a cappella Prayer of Consolation underscored hope and meaning in the midst of tragedy. Within one short month, Nick compiled the scripture text and composed the music. On the first anniversary of 9/11, a professional choir performed Prayer of Consolation in the Washington National Cathedral as part of the official commemoration. I am sure God was pleased.

The Bible is history, prophecy, teaching, and poetry. It is useful in tragedy and in ordinary times. It helps you find your voice. It is gives you words to pray, sing, or cry. Better still, when you listen closely, you can hear God speak to your cherished heart. He knows you: where you have been, where you are, and where you are going. First He moves you heart, and then He moves your feet. It isn't a "chicken and egg" question of which one comes first. Feet often follow the dictates of the heart. God wants to possess your heart so that you fall in love, leap into faith, and run to tell others.

As a warm-up, tune your heart to His and get ready to fall into the rhythm of following Him. In this devotion, listen to God before you act. Ask Him to help you find your voice in harmony with Him. Ask Him to align your footwork to His.

WALKING: Reading the notes

This devotion could be staged as a musical. It is a conversation that begins and ends with a confession of your need for God. As such, it is a model for prayer.

As you read through the first time, think of yourself as a member of the chorus. Pay attention to your cues and your lines. Underline all the footwork terms, and circle all the references that describe or express the heart. Read the verses slowly and let the meanings sink in.

On your second reading, notice how in tune the chorus is to God's heart. Beside each other verse, note whether you hear harmony or disharmony. Is the footwork in accord? (A little time back stage would reveal how consistent the performers are in real life.)

It is time to practice on your own before God as your audience. Read the Prelude, then the Chorus lines and finally the Postlude aloud. Pause after each verse, adding some details about your attitude and the way you use your feet. Most importantly, let the practice time be a dialogue between you and the Holy Spirit as your director. This will help you learn your lines by heart before you walk on.

FOLLOWING THROUGH: Improvising your part

Memorizing is a first step toward improvising. You concentrate on learning until it becomes natural. God wants His Word, His expressions, to become the expressions of your heart. As this devotion illustrates, His model for coordinating heart and soles is a dialogue that builds toward the crescendo of love and faith. Your feet coordinate with your heart in a conscious outward expression of an inward relationship with God.

In "improv", seasoned actors act without a script. A simple rule of improvisation or "jamming" (to use the musical vernacular) is to follow through with what you have just heard, taking the action in a new direction. Improvisation is what the Holy Spirit does for you, in you, and through you as you live life and interact with others. The people you meet need to see their lives reflected in what you say. Each time, you will need to improvise. Tune your heart to Him and watch your feet do what Jesus would do.

11

The Prime Mover

The expression "Let go and let God" declares that God can do what you cannot. In this devotion, you contemplate God as the source of your strength, and the one who enables you to move forward.

Jeremiah 10:23 (NLT)

I know, LORD, that our lives are not our own. We are not able to plan our own course.

Job 13:27 (NIV 1984)

You fasten my feet in shackles; you keep close watch on all my paths by putting marks on the soles of my feet.

Job 31:4 (NKJV)

Does He not see my ways, And count all my steps?

Isaiah 40:29–31 (NLT)

He gives power to the weak and strength to the powerless. Even youths will become weak and tired, and young men will fall in exhaustion. But those who trust in the LORD will find new strength. They will soar high on wings like eagles. They will run and not grow weary. They will walk and not faint.

Zechariah 10:12 (NIV 1984)

"I will strengthen them in the LORD and in his name they will walk," declares the LORD.

Habakkuk 3:19 (NIV 1984)

The Sovereign LORD is my strength; he makes my feet like the feet of a deer, he enables me to go on the heights.

Acts 17:28a (NIV 1984)

"For in him we live and move and have our being."

ENTERING: Who is at the center?

Galileo proved the theory that the earth revolves around the sun. Difficult to accept at first, this proof changed everyone's worldview. Later, astronomers identified galaxies beyond what they could see. These discoveries mirror human maturation as it unfolds from childhood to adulthood. You and I began life with the illusion of being at its center. Eventually, disappointments and the divine bring perspective. God is the sovereign center of life, the prime mover of everything and everyone.

The age-old battle for the cherished center of your child-like heart continues. Every day, what you want and what you have to do commands attention. Distractions and demands are the idols that displace God's place of priority. They dupe you into thinking that your hopes, happiness, and heartbreaks are at the center of the universe.

Before entering this devotion, bow to the Lord of all universes. Surrender your life in faith to the One who moved heaven and earth to be with you.

WALKING: Who is in control?

As you walk through the verses for the first time, take Jesus' hand. Look into His face and close your eyes before you begin. Think about what you are like and what He is like. Ask Him to reveal His all-powerful and ever-present nature.

As you go through, find one phrase that moves your heart, and underline it. Look into His face again and use that phrase in a short prayer.

Create a chart before your second reading. Draw three columns down two pages. Jeremiah 10:23 gets the top line of this exercise. In the first column write "My life is not my own." In the second column, "I am not able to plan my own course." Leave the third column blank for now.

As you walk through again, read each verse and look for evidence or support for the assertion at the top of the page. Draw a line to separate each verse entry. Imagine God speaking this truth about life to you. Use simple, child-friendly words.

For Isaiah 40:29–31, I wrote:
God helps me when I feel tired. He gets me moving again.
For Acts 17:28a, I wrote:
My life is in Him. He is central. I move as He moves.

Continue filling in this chart for all of the verses. Notice that God can be your source for the physical, psychological, and spiritual choices you (unconsciously) make when you move. Think of Him as the source of your breath, strength, wisdom, and power. Underlying these verses is His love for you.

Read the verses one last time. Let Jesus speak each one as a declaration of God's love for you.

FOLLOWING THROUGH: Who is releasing control?

It is time for a little introspection. How is God moving in the middle of your life today? Complete the top of the third column on your chart with the phrase from the beginning of Jeremiah 10:23: "I know, Lord." (I can't see You, but on faith, I know, Lord).

At each verse pause with eyes closed. Let the Holy Spirit remind you of a circumstance. To make it memorable, write a word or two to name it in the margin. Ask God for strength, wisdom, and power through His Spirit to release control to Him in that circumstance. Declare in prayer that God is the prime mover in your life.

12

Standing Firm

Standing firmly in one place is difficult. Physically, pain and impatience vie for your attention. Spiritually, your enemy mistakes your stability for inability. He's wrong: standing firmly is a still-life representation of animate faith. Sometimes, in your spiritual walk, standing is the strongest position you can take.

Isaiah 7:9b (NLT)

Unless your faith is firm, I cannot make you stand firm.

Exodus 14:13b (NIV 1984)

"Do not be afraid. Stand firm and you will see the deliverance the Lord will bring you today."

Matthew 10:22 (NIV 1984)

All men will hate you because of me, but he who stands firm to the end will be saved.

Luke 21:19 (NIV 1984)

By standing firm you will gain life.

1 Corinthians 15:58 (NIV 1984)

Therefore, my dear brothers, stand firm. Let nothing move you. Always give yourselves fully to the work of the Lord, because you know that your labor in the Lord is not in vain.

1 Corinthians 16:13 (NIV 1984)

Be on your guard; stand firm in the faith; be men of courage; be strong.

Ephesians 6:13 (NLT)

Put on every piece of God's armor so you will be able to resist the enemy in the time of evil. Then after the battle you will still be standing firm.

Philippians 1:27 (NIV 1984)

Whatever happens, conduct yourselves in a manner worthy of the gospel of Christ... I will know that you stand firm in one spirit, contending as one man for the faith of the gospel

James 5:8 (NIV 1984)

You too, be patient and stand firm, because the Lord's coming is near.

1 Peter 5:9a (NLT)

Stand firm against [the devil], and be strong in your faith.

ENTERING: Fixed feet

Imagine a public place where people are standing or milling about, going about their business. Suddenly, one after the other, join in a "flash mob," a choreographed dance. It catches onlookers by surprise. Worldwide, flash mobs are proliferating, with many celebrating Christ through movement. YouTube captures people going from an inconspicuous state to an all-out faith fest. Thousands in Hungary dance in a main plaza at Easter to celebrate their risen King. Thousands in Holland hold placards sending love and prayers to the Japanese suffering from natural disasters; they form a group picture of a heart. Flash mobs coordinate the seemingly inanimate into an animated message.

Standing firm as a Christ-follower is comparable. Your spiritual position is a statement of faith in Jesus. Standing firm is stillness, an inconspicuous condition of rest born of the assurance that the Spirit of God is moving in and around you. As and when the Holy Spirit initiates, you fall into coordinated step with Him. Your feet are not planted, they are poised. "Stand firm" is an admonition to watch what He is doing and to wait on Him to lead. It is a world-wide movement of the feet and faith of the Body of Christ. It catches the enemy off guard.

This devotion helps you understand how all of this happens. There is order: having a firm faith precedes being able to stand firm. There is also orchestration: only Jesus can make your faith firm, and only Jesus can help you stand firm. He is the head of His body.

WALKING: Fixed faith

Jesus is the author and perfecter of your faith; the key is to fix your eyes on Him (Hebrews 12:2). As you begin this devotion, ask the Holy Spirit to increase your concentration on Jesus. On your first reading of all the verses keep this in mind: Isaiah 7:9b sets up two consistent factors to watch for:

- Unless your faith is firm
- [God] cannot make you stand firm.

And since we know that Jesus is the one making your faith firm, He is the One making you stand firm.

On your second reading, imagine that the passages describe where you are at, spiritually. Ask Jesus to help you discover your faith and feet equilibrium.

1. Underline all the phrases related to "standing firm." That's a picture of you, being stable and certain of the truth of the gospel of Jesus Christ.
2. Make a list of what is happening around your firmly planted feet. For example, in Exodus, "you will see deliverance." Some of what is happening around you will be invisible. These include enabling, eternal life, fruitful labor, protection, salvation, unity, spiritual battles, etc.

There are many unseen ways that God moves. Faith is being certain of what you do not see (Hebrews 11:1b, NIV 1984). Jesus is in charge of everything, seen and unseen.

On your third reading, find God's commands that will help you stand firm. Remember, He is the One who will enable you to obey. Match each of the following commands to the verse it comes from. Whether the verse is warning you or encouraging you, remember that He asks this of you because He wants to do it for you:

*   Be courageous.
*   Be on your guard.
*   Be patient.
*   Be strong.
*   Beware that all men will hate you because of Jesus.
*   Conduct yourself in a manner worthy of the gospel.
*   Contend for the gospel.
*   Do not be afraid.
*   Give yourself fully.
*   Let nothing move you.

Beside each of these, write your estimate of how you fare on a scale of 1–10. You may give yourself fully (so, maybe you are 9), but you know you are not particularly courageous (so maybe, you are a 2). Some people may think you are patient, but you know better (so maybe, you are a 5). On the basis of this scale, decide what improvement or building up of your faith to ask Jesus for. Hebrews 11:1 also says that "Faith is being sure of what we hope for." Let yourself freely hope for improvement in your faith and in your certainty that Jesus is able and active in your life.

As you stand in obedience, your faith is in balance. Standing firm is a ready position for faithful feet to get on the move.

FOLLOWING THROUGH: Fixed Hope

What do you do if you are no longer standing firm? How do you get back on your feet? Or how do you advise and encourage a friend who has slipped and fallen? Remember, from start to finish it is Jesus who helps you. Hang on to this additional verse:

He lifted me out of the slimy pit, out of the mud and mire; he set my feet on a rock and gave me a firm place to stand. (Psalm 40:2, NIV 1984)

Ask God to make this verse a reality in your life.

13

Walking in Obedience

God commands that you walk in obedience to Him but He never insists on it. In this devotion, you explore how to make His commands for your feet the desire of your heart.

Jeremiah 6:16 (NIV 1984)

This is what the LORD says: "Stand at the crossroads and look; ask for the ancient paths, ask where the good way is, and walk in it, and you will find rest for your souls."

Deuteronomy 5:33 (NKJV)

You shall walk in all the ways which the LORD your God has commanded you, that you may live and that I may be well with you, and that you may prolong your days in the land which you shall possess.

Deuteronomy 10:12 (NIV 1984)

And now, O Israel, what does the LORD your God ask of you but to fear the LORD your God, to walk in all his ways, to love him, to serve the LORD your God with all your heart and with all your soul?

Deuteronomy 11:22 (NLT)

"Be careful to obey all these commands I am giving you. Show love to the LORD your God by walking in his ways and holding tightly to him."

Isaiah 30:21 (NIV 1984)

Whether you turn to the right or to the left, your ears will hear a voice behind you, saying, "This is the way; walk in it."

Colossians 3:6b, 7 (NKJV)

The wrath of God is coming upon the sons of disobedience, in which you yourselves once walked when you lived with them.

2 John 1:6 (NIV 1984)

And this is love: that we walk in obedience to his commands. As you have heard from the beginning, his command is that you walk in love.

ENTERING: Duty or desire

I grew up on a daily diet of religious schools and a weekly dose of church. During the service, my attention often wandered from God: checking out altar boys, people- and clock-watching, and dreaming about other spiritual avenues. As a teen, I became a regular at Baha'i meetings and read about Baba Ram Das, a spiritual icon of the era. Song lyrics and poetry were the words that ascribed meaning to my life. Later, as a traveler, I sought solace in empty temples and meditated in even emptier Zen gardens. Swept up by the supernatural, I even sought out psychics and astrologists. I really wandered from God. On reflection, I think I was looking for hope in all the wrong places.

When I sought out Jesus years later, I was different. He was the same, just a lot more interesting. At first, my passion for Him was on a low burner with a steady pilot light. At one point, I remember saying, "God, I won't be able to 'do duty' but I will 'do desire.'" He turned up the fire. He kindled my faith. Suddenly, I wanted what He wanted.

How do you get "desire"? You ask God for it. This simple request was not clear to me when I was young. Desire had a different connotation to me. And duty, well, it numbed my inner spirit. I doubted that anyone would want to become more dutiful. But now, I see beauty in every simple act of obedience to God.

Hold duty and desire in tension as you go through these scriptures.

WALKING: Obedience with benefits

This collection of scripture begins with the reading from Jeremiah, because it challenges you to find your feet at your crossroads. What are the circumstances, the choices you are facing? Using this verse, ask God to show you the good path to follow.

Now read the whole collection again, imagining God the Father addressing you by name as His child. Personalize the pronouns. Do you hear His loving tones connecting what He requires along with what He will give? Underline the commands and double underline the promises. Use your pencil again to circle the word "if" in these verses. Why do you think God commands you to walk in His ways? Couldn't He just ask you?

Read through one more time. Are you surprised how many promises He is making? Try drawing a mind map using these verses. Draw a circle with "obey" and "walk in God's ways" in the center. Write all the promises from these verses, placing them around the circle.

Reflect on which verses inspire duty or desire in you to obey.

FOLLOWING THROUGH: Submission

How does God prompt you to obedience? Does He nudge your conscience, or place niggling thoughts in your mind? Does He use His word to speak to you? Or trusted friends to advise you? Examine how open your heart is to His encouragement. When you have a sense of His direction, do you respond out of duty or desire?

Consider how Isaiah describes God's Spirit as the enabler of an obedient walk. He directs your feet saying: "This is the way walk in it." He doesn't insist; He is a gentleman.

Spend a few minutes in silence, asking Him to tune your inner spirit to His Spirit today. Ask Him to give you a burning desire to follow His ways. Ask Him for a transformed, sweetly submissive heart. Bow your head before your God. Go low.

IV

Protection and Foot Care–
Receiving God's Touch

14

Foot Coverings

Shoes tell stories about the wearer. The footwear of a ballerina, a welder, or a nurse is distinct; shoes symbolize stories of the life lived in them. Between the lines is a spiritual narrative: God designed foot coverings to tell His story.

Exodus 12:11 (NLT)

These are your instructions for eating this meal: Be fully dressed, wear your sandals, and carry your walking stick in your hand. Eat the meal with urgency, for this is the LORD's Passover.

Deuteronomy 25:9, 10 (NLT)

The widow must walk over to him in the presence of the elders, pull his sandal from his foot, and spit in his face. Then she must declare, "This is what happens to a man who refuses to provide his brother with children." Ever afterward in Israel his family will be referred to as "the family of the man whose sandal was pulled off."

Deuteronomy 29:5 (NKJV)

And I have led you forty years in the wilderness. Your clothes have not worn out on you, and your sandals have not worn out on your feet.

Ruth 4:7, 8 (NLT)

Now in those days it was the custom in Israel for anyone transferring a right of purchase to remove his sandal and hand it to the other party. This publicly validated the transaction. So the other family redeemer drew off his sandal as he said to Boaz, "You buy the land."

Psalm 60:8b (NIV 1984)

Upon Edom I toss my sandal.

Matthew 3:11 (NKJV)

I indeed baptize you with water unto repentance, but He who is coming after me is mightier than I, whose sandals I am not worthy to carry. He will baptize you with the Holy Spirit and fire.

Luke 15:22 (NKJV) [The parable of the prodigal son]

But the father said to his servants, "Bring out the best robe and put it on him, and put a ring on his hand and sandals on his feet."

Ephesians 6:13, 15 (NLT)

Therefore, put on every piece of God's armor so you will be able to resist the enemy in the time of evil. Then after the battle, you will be standing firm.... For shoes, put on the peace that comes from the Good News, so that you will be fully prepared.

ENTERING: Barefoot symbolism

Think back to the story of the Garden of Eden in Genesis. Adam and Eve were free, naked, unashamed, and living with God. Being naked presumes they were barefoot. Then they sinned against God and everything was different; they were restricted, naked, and ashamed. Still barefoot, they heard God's warning that their new-found "frenemy" would soon be attacking their feet (Genesis 3:15).

Before expelling them from His presence, God performed the first-ever blood sacrifice of animals to clothe Adam and Eve. It is not clear if that included footwear. But God sent them out into the world (Genesis 3:21, 23). This story foreshadows the symbolism of sacrifice: the spiritual covering of sin that caused separation from the presence of God. It also asserts that God had a plan to crush the enemy under His feet.

In the meantime, Adam and Eve – footloose and vulnerable – had to watch out for physical and spiritual hazards as they tried to survive on their own. The Bible describes the next generations wearing shoes, sandals, and boots. Footwear would always be doubly significant: estrangement from God and His provision to protect. Before entering this devotion, thank God that He has you covered from head to toe.

WALKING: Foot-covering symbolism

On your first reading of these verses, underline every mention of footwear. Then assess whether any of the verses and their back stories are unfamiliar. If one is, as a first step, read the Bible chapter the story comes from. This will help you understand the symbolism of the footwear. For example, in Matthew 3, John the Baptist is the speaker. His reference to Jesus' sandal is a spiritual revelation about Jesus to his listeners.

Second time around, ask the Holy Spirit to help you match the verse and its mention of foot coverings to the following possible symbolic meanings:

- being ready to depart when the enemy attacks
- claiming possession of someone else's territory
- having humility in the presence of God
- identifying broken relationships
- receiving supernatural protection
- restoring a relationship with God the Father
- transferring ownership of land
- walking in the peace of God's good news

Ponder each verse and its symbolism – what it might represent in God's story of love and redemption after sin befell His children. These verses reveal His character throughout: faithfulness, mercy, sovereignty, humility, and peacefulness. Can you see yourself or your relationship with God in any of these verses?

FOLLOWING THROUGH: "To cover or not to cover" symbolism

If you read between the lines, you will see God is using shoes again in this story.

A million Ethiopians, according to Christianity Today magazine (May 2011), suffer from a debilitating foot disease called "podoconiosis" or "podo" for short. It severely deforms and immobilizes feet. Barefoot farmers and their families on volcanic soils are the most vulnerable. Christian researchers, doctors, and nuns have pooled their knowledge and are successfully treating "podo" sufferers. In one sense, it is an uphill battle because farmers who wear shoes are considered to be lazy, but they are coming around to understand that foot washing and shoe-wearing are what prevents and even cures "podo." A Christian shoe company is also part of the recovery campaign.

After reading this article, I had the privilege of visiting a treatment site and a custom boot factory in Northern Ethiopia operated by the Ethiopian Orthodox Christian Charity. Eye-opening and humbling don't even begin to describe what I received. I only hope I walked away changed.

What strikes you about this story? Can you see the symbolism?

15

Foot Washing

In picking up a towel and a basin to wash their feet, Jesus took on the role of servant to His disciples. Through foot washing, the disciples discovered that they had a lot to learn about the depth of Jesus' servant love for them.

John 13:1–17 (NIV 1984)

It was just before the Passover Feast. Jesus knew that the time had come for him to leave this world and go to the Father. Having loved his own who were in the world, he now showed them the full extent of his love. The evening meal was being served, and the devil had already prompted Judas Iscariot, son of Simon, to betray Jesus.

Jesus knew that the Father had put all things under his power, and that he had come from God and was returning to God; so he got up from the meal, took off his outer clothing, and wrapped a towel around his waist. After that, he poured water into a basin, and began to wash his disciples' feet, drying them with the towel that was wrapped around him.

He came to Simon Peter, who said to him, "Lord, are you going to wash my feet?" Jesus replied, "You do not realize now what I am doing, but later you will understand." "No," said Peter, "you shall never wash my feet." Jesus answered, "Unless I wash you, you have no part with me." "Then, Lord," Simon Peter replied, "Not just my feet but my hands and my head as well!"

Jesus answered, "A person who has had a bath needs only to wash his feet; his whole body is clean. And you are clean, though not every one of you." For he knew who was going to betray him, and that was why he said not every one was clean.

When he had finished washing their feet, he put on his clothes and returned to his place. "Do you understand what I have done for you?" He asked them. "You call me 'Teacher' and 'Lord,' and rightly so, for that is what I am. Now that I, your Lord and Teacher, have washed your feet, you should also wash one another's feet. I have set you an example that you should do as I have done for you.

I tell you the truth, no servant is greater than his master, nor is a messenger greater than the one who sent him. Now that you know these things, you will be blessed if you do them."

ENTERING: Foresight

On the eve of His crucifixion, Jesus knew what was coming. His disciples' lives were about to change; human history was at a turning point. Surprisingly, Jesus chose to wash His disciples' feet at their last gathering.

Foot washing was a customary practice in the Middle East in Jesus' day. A house servant would wash the dust and grime from the feet of sandal-wearing guests. It was both hospitable and healthy. Why would Jesus have chosen a routine task normally performed by a lowly person? Was He trying to prepare His disciples for what they would misconstrue as a future without Him?

Bow your head and, before you close your eyes, look at your feet. God wants to prepare you for something, too. Ask the Holy Spirit to show you His heavenly intentions on the horizon of your life.

WALKING: Insight

Have you ever had your feet washed by someone else? Or have you washed the feet of a friend or a stranger? Foot washing is an intimate act that can prompt very personal topics of conversation. People rarely talk about their feet, but most have feelings about them. Foot washing can bring those feelings to the surface.

First, read the passage entirely from Jesus' point of view. Step into His shoes. Know what He knows; do what He does; ask what He asks. To help you – remember that He knows

- that He is the Son of God and His time on earth is ending
- what is in Judas's heart
- what is hindering His disciples' faith in Him
- what is going to happen when He leaves their gathering
- that the Passover meal foreshadows the heavenly significance of what will happen next in His life

What does Jesus do with the disciples' feet? How did He explain what He was doing? What did He mean by clean bodies and dirty feet?

Now, read the passage entirely from the disciples' perspective. Peter voiced their concerns, and Judas may have misunderstood what was happening. You can choose to reread it from either perspective. How would you describe their reactions to their Lord and Master washing their feet? Alarmed? Confused? Self-conscious?

When Peter protested, Jesus answered that foot washing was essential to identifying with Him. Do you think the disciples understood the cleansing as Jesus intended? As part of their lesson, He challenged them to do what He had done, to wash each other's feet. This was very counter-cultural. They were probably humbled and mystified. None of them knew what the next day held or what its world-changing effect would be. Not yet.

Finally, read the passage from your own viewpoint – that of a post-crucifixion believer in Jesus. What difference does knowing what would happen next make? Think about the ways Jesus exercised His love.

FOLLOWING THROUGH: Clear sight

Let Jesus, in His mercy, wash your feet. Imagine Him kneeling before you, holding your feet. Imagine the love expressed in His eyes.

The water in the basin unexpectedly buoys your feet. They are weightless and floating. You feel His hands – cool and refreshing. The water releases and disperses the dust from your feet. It is a heavenly feeling. The water cools the heat from the road and the blisters from your shoes.

Your brokenness – feet and heart alike – empty into and are filled by this water. No longer maimed, they move only as His hand directs. Every part of your foot re-forms to His hands.

Immersed, washed clean, and towel-dried, you are feet-ready and heart-worthy for the road again. Your message-carrying feet are prepared by heaven to walk on earth. You can now wash another person's feet.

Empty the basin. Note what the water has taken with it.

16

Guarding your Feet

When you walk with God, you can rest assured that He "has" your feet.
Your challenge is to remember that no matter where you go.

Deuteronomy 2:7 (NLT)

*For the LORD your God has blessed you in everything you have done. He
has watched your every step through this great wilderness.*

1 Samuel 2:9 (NKJV)

He will guard the feet of His saints.

2 Samuel 22:37 (MSG)

You cleared the ground under me so my footing was firm.

Psalm 1:6 (NLT)

The LORD watches over the path of the godly.

Psalm 91:11, 12 (NIV 1984)

For he will command his angels concerning you to guard you in all your ways; they will lift you up in their hands, so that you will not strike your foot against a stone.

Psalm 94:17–19 (NIV 1984)

Unless the LORD had given me help, I would soon have dwelt in the silence of death. When I said, "My foot is slipping," your love, O LORD, supported me. When anxiety was great within me, your consolation brought joy to my soul.

Psalm 121:2, 3 (NIV 1984)

My help comes from the LORD, the Maker of heaven and earth. He will not let your foot slip— he who watches over you will not slumber.

ENTERING: Moving from fear to peace

In this world, resting and remembering are not the usual strategies for handling fear of the unknown. Instead, people buy locks, avoid eye contact, and check safety warranties.

God's specific words in the Bible help you transition from fear to peace; He is guarding your very feet. He assures you of His presence, protection, and overcoming power. He can see what you can't. Taking your eyes off distressing situations and putting them on Him would enable you to step courageously onto His path.

Resting in God means you trust Him to take care of you. Remember who He is – the all-seeing God of the universe. He has heaven's perspective on the road ahead. How do you shift your focus from earthly to heavenly things? You need God's help to figure out why trusting Him is difficult for you. With the Holy Spirit leading you, name situations that might frighten you: uncharted relationships, money or marriage troubles, parenting or interpersonal conflicts, job or health issues. Confess your fears to God. Pour out your heart. As you draw near to Him, He draws even closer to you.

If you are able, go now into a room alone and close the door. Take off your shoes. Close your eyes. Ask God to touch your mind with the peace of Christ Jesus. Ask Him to anoint your heart and your feet with oil, representing the Holy Spirit. Imagine Him writing Jesus' name with the oil. You belong to Him. He is going to change the way you walk by showing you that He has you covered.

WALKING: Receiving and repeating assurance

Scan the verses all the way through, underlining all the words that relate to guarding, protection, safety, watching, supporting, and any words of assurance that catch your eye. This will give you a sense of which verses you want to go back to.

Now read the verses out loud in a gentle voice. Without thinking too much about the words, let them enter and replace the worries that dwell in your heart. Ask Jesus to clear the awful fear that has invaded your heart so that you can receive the assurance of His protection. Ask Him to help you trust Him, to increase your faith.

As you review, select two or three verses that you want to spend time pondering and repeating. Take as much time with this contemplation as you can. Think of God's Word as flowers and yourself as the hummingbird drawing nourishment from them. Draw strength, courage, and comfort – anything that God offers you in assurance.

Now, as you walk out of that room into the circumstances of your life, you know where to focus your eyes, don't you? You won't see Him but He is guarding you. And you know what to remember as you walk. You can rest in God, as you move with Him in His unforced rhythms of grace.

FOLLOWING THROUGH: Remembering God's words to you

Now, if you could only carry these verses with you into daily life. There are lots of ways to keep focused on the unseen life you have in Christ.

Memorize a verse and hide it in your heart.
- Write verses on Post-it notes and recipe cards and put them on the bathroom mirror and car dashboard.
- Put your smart phone and lap top to good use to assist you.
- Go the low-tech route of our ancestors of faith: write the verses on the bottom of your shoes or put them on paper inside your shoes. How many pairs of shoes do you have? Just think of the possibilities!
- God has you covered, not to mention the road ahead of you.

17

The Lame Walk

One of the most beautiful images of Jesus extending love on earth is in His healing of the lame. The Old Testament associates this healing with the restoration of relationship. Jesus didn't disagree.

Old Testament prophecies:

Jeremiah 31:7–9 (NLT)

Now this is what the LORD says: "Sing with joy for Israel.... For I will bring them from the north and from the distant corners of the earth. I will not forget the blind and lame, the expectant mothers and women in labor. A great company will return!

Tears of joy will stream down their faces, and I will lead them home with great care. They will walk beside quiet streams and on smooth paths where they will not stumble."

Micah 4:5–7 (NIV)

We will walk in the name of the LORD our God for ever and ever.

"In that day," declares the LORD, "I will gather the lame; I will assemble the exiles and those I have brought to grief. I will make the lame my

remnant, those driven away a strong nation. The LORD will rule over them in Mount Zion from that day and forever."

During Jesus' earthly ministry:

Luke 5:21–25 (NIV 1984)

The Pharisees and the teachers of the law began thinking to themselves, "Who is this fellow who speaks blasphemy? Who can forgive sins but God alone?" Jesus knew what they were thinking and asked, "Why are you thinking these things in your hearts? Which is easier: to say, 'Your sins are forgiven,' or to say, 'Get up and walk'? But that you may know that the Son of Man has authority on earth to forgive sins…" He said to the paralyzed man, "I tell you, get up, take your mat and go home." Immediately he stood up in front of them, took what he had been lying on and went home praising God.

Luke 7:20–23 (NLT)

John's two disciples found Jesus and said to Him, "John the Baptist sent us to ask, 'Are you the Messiah we've been expecting, or should we keep looking for someone else?'"

At that very time, Jesus cured many people of their diseases, illnesses, and evil spirits and restored sight to many who were blind. Then He told John's disciples, "Go back to John and tell him what you have seen and heard – the blind see, the lame walk, the lepers are cured, the deaf hear, the dead are raised to life, and the Good News is being preached to the poor. And tell him, 'God blesses those who do not turn away because of Me.'"

After Jesus' resurrection and ascension

Acts 3:2, 4, 6–8 (NIV)

Now a man who was lame from birth was being carried to the temple gate called Beautiful, where he was put every day to beg from those going into the temple courts.... Peter looked straight at him, as did John. Then Peter said, "Look at us!"

...Then Peter said, "Silver or gold I do not have, but what I do have I give you. In the name of Jesus Christ of Nazareth, walk." Taking him by the right hand, he helped him up, and instantly the man's feet and ankles became strong. He jumped to his feet and began to walk. Then he went with them into the temple courts, walking and jumping, and praising God.

Acts 14:8–10 (NLT)

While they were at Lystra, Paul and Barnabas came upon a man with crippled feet. He had been that way from birth, so he had never walked. He was sitting and listening as Paul preached. Looking straight at him, Paul realized he had faith to be healed. So Paul called to him in a loud voice, "Stand up!" And the man jumped to his feet and started walking.

ENTERING: Royal treatment

Mephibosheth[1] is introduced in 2 Samuel chapters 4 and 9 as a grandson of King Saul. He was lame in both feet, having fallen as a child. At the time of the account, it was a politically intense period in the kingdom and he went into hiding. He had assumed that David, now on the throne, was his enemy. Quite unexpectedly, King David sent for Mephibosheth, asking his servant to carry the lame boy back to the palace. Misunderstanding the king's purpose, Mephibosheth cowered in

---

[1]   Charles Stanley, Mephibosheth, lame on both feet or, the Kindness of God (Bible Centre; 2006 Oct. http://www.biblecentre.org/topics/chst_mephiposheth.htm)

his presence. But David honored the young man as a full member of the royal household – no conditions attached. Mephibosheth was treated as a son joining in at the banquet table. His lame feet were under the "all you can eat" table and His eyes were on the king.

Pastor and author Charles Stanley suggests that the Mephibosheth story parallels the one in the Garden of Eden. The comparable "fallen" condition of Adam and Eve prompts them to hide (Genesis 3:8). They and their descendants (you and I) depend on God's rescue and restoration to His family. Like Mephibosheth, we are invited to dine at the table of the King of Kings. Our celebration of Holy Communion foreshadows this royal banquet. We, like Mephibosheth, have a rightful place at the table when relationship with the King is restored.

Bow your head with me. Ask God to prepare your heart for what He wants to show you in this devotion. Ask Him to correct any misconceptions you have about being lame – either physically or spiritually. Thank Him for the invitation to dine together.

WALKING: Heavenly gait

God's character traits of mercy and grace are on full display throughout these verses. His compassion permeates the scenes. As you read through the scripture for the first time, underline the places where you sense God's mercy and grace. What do you think about the scale of God's promises to heal the lame?

Start your second reading with Luke 5. Then go through the rest of the verses and contemplate Jesus' comparison of spiritual sin and physical paralysis. Do you think receiving forgiveness and receiving physical healing are similar? Would you accept that since the Fall in the Garden of Eden we are all spiritually lame? Does sin immobilize you and affect your walk with God? As you read these verses, ask the Holy Spirit to touch you with God's mercy and grace.

"The Lame Walk" devotion is full of action. On your final reading, go slowly and pause after each verse. With your eyes closed, replay each scene in your imagination. Keep your focus on the footwork. A lot of spirited movement is condensed into simple words:

- "Assemble" – imagine the sounds of shuffling feet.
- "Get up" – think of the excitement of being on his feet for the first time.
- "Walking and jumping" – that's not temple decorum, I'm sure.

Are those who are physically lame an object lesson, a concrete illustration, of being spiritually lame? Reflect on your spiritual walk with God. Are you crippled by bitterness? By fear? By an unforgiving heart? What is your spiritual limp?

Shift your focus back to those who have physically disabled footwork. Think how injuries cause people to temporarily limp, or how those afflicted with cerebral palsy drag their feet, or how the gait of a war vet changes with a new prosthetic. Do these examples of footwork demonstrate dependence, humility, and courage? What do they teach you about the Kingdom of God? Shifting between the physical and spiritual parallels gets easier the more you do it.

When Jesus came to walk in this world and in your shoes, His dusty feet felt every bump on the road. He even took nails in His feet, retaining the marks of His suffering after His resurrection. He made a way for the lame to walk – He walked the talk.

FOLLOWING THROUGH: Kingdom gate

The Lame Walk is a powerful picture of God's Kingdom on earth. As a footwork metaphor, it uses disabled feet to show you God's healing – physically and spiritually – and to remind you of your restoration to the family of God.

Most people who walked through the Beautiful Gate at the Temple would have ignored the beggar, his feet tucked under and hands outstretched. But God saw him. He saw a perfect opportunity to show His loving power. Peter and John took notice and obeyed the prompting of God's Spirit. Everyone, even the passersby, got a glimpse of God's Kingdom that day.

Park yourself near a gate soon. It might be a gate to your children's playground, the lobby of an office building, or an entrance to a mall.

Observe the diverse footwork through God's eyes of grace and mercy. Silently proclaim God's plans and promises of healing and restoration through Jesus Christ, physically and spiritually, on each life you see. "Thy Kingdom come, Thy will be done."

18

Miracles on Foot

Among the many spiritual influences in society are those that endow nature with supernatural qualities. The Creator plays a lesser role to creation or creatures. This devotion offers snippets of stories about human feet encountering the Creator's power. These miracles declare who rightly deserves your worship.

Psalm 66:6 (NKJV)

He turned the sea into dry land; they went through the river on foot.

Hebrews 11:29 (MSG)

By an act of faith, Israel walked through the Red Sea on dry ground. The Egyptians tried it and drowned.

Deuteronomy 29:5 (NKJV)

And I have led you forty years in the wilderness. Your clothes have not worn out on you, and your sandals have not worn out on your feet.

Joshua 3:13, 17 (NLT)

The priests will carry the Ark of the LORD, the Lord of all the earth. As soon as their feet touch the water, the flow of the water will be cut off upstream, and the river will stand up like a wall....Meanwhile, the priests who were carrying the Ark of the Lord's Covenant stood on dry ground in the middle of the riverbed as the people passed by. They waited there until the whole nation of Israel had crossed the Jordan on dry ground.

2 Kings 2:8 (MSG)

Elijah took his cloak, rolled it up, and hit the water with it. The river divided and the two men walked through on dry land.

Daniel 3:22–25 (NIV 1984)

The king's command was so urgent and the furnace so hot that the flames of the fire killed the soldiers who took [the three men] ... into the blazing furnace. Then King Nebuchadnezzar leaped to his feet in amazement and asked his advisers, "Weren't there three men that we tied up and threw into the fire?" They replied, "Certainly, O king." He said, "Look! I see four men walking around in the fire, unbound and unharmed, and the fourth looks like a son of the gods."

Mark 6:47–50 (NLT)

Late that night, the disciples were in their boat in the middle of the lake, and Jesus was alone on the land. He saw that they were in serious trouble, rowing hard and struggling against the wind and waves. About three o'clock in the morning, Jesus came toward them, walking on the water. He intended to go past them, but when they saw him walking on the water, they cried out in terror, thinking he was a ghost. They were all terrified when they saw him. But Jesus spoke to them at once. "Don't be afraid," he said, "Take courage. I am here!"

ENTERING: Elementary exposure

The veneration of the elements – air, water, earth, and fire – occurs in Zoroastrianism, Hinduism, Buddhism, shamanism, Wicca, astrology, and tarot-reading. Adherents derive understandings of the intricate interconnectedness of creation and explain supernatural power through the elements themselves. These beliefs have crept into western culture with the popularization of yoga and other normalized eastern practices. It even shows up in advertising. Consider the spiritual aspects of this sandal advertisement from juil.com:

"Do more than walk. Connect. Rebalance natural energies. Rediscover true comfort. Relish everyone's compliments. Our exclusive conductors connect you to the earth with every step you take… Awaken your soles." …The term "New Age" describes this spiritual movement.

As you prepare to read scripture, bow your head and heart to Jesus, King and Creator, of whom His disciples exclaimed, *"What kind of man is this? Even the winds and the waves obey him!"* (Matthew 8:27, NIV). In this devotion, human feet actively discover God's miraculous power over nature. Keep your heart tucked in; there could be some spiritual headwinds.

WALKING: Secondary examination

The Spirit of God who lives within you accompanies you everywhere. Ask Him to go before you in this devotion, leading you.

First, read each verse, underlining the words or phrases that refer to one of the four elements. You will find wind, river, dry ground, furnace, and many others. Write the names of the corresponding elements in the margin: air, water, earth, fire.

As you go through the second time, circle references to triumphant or even tentative footwork in each verse. For example, travel, on foot, stood, etc. Stop and think. Can you imagine being in that death-defying situation? God wants you to share in His constant victory; identify what the impossible was in each verse. For example: surviving in a fire, walking through a sea, not having shoes wear out during forty years in the wilderness. With the Holy Spirit's leading, make a declaration of

God's power over the natural impossibility in each verse. Say aloud to yourself, "God was victorious over (what was impossible for humans); He commanded (whatever element)."

What is the first "impossible" thing that comes to your mind that you would ask God to do in your life? Ask Him. Don't be shy; He is the One who can override human nature and all of nature. Now reread the verses, and ask Jesus, "the author and perfecter of your faith," to read them with you. Ask again, at a higher tempo of faith.

FOLLOWING THROUGH: Primary focus

The enemy of God, "the prince of the air," has wily ways. You can see that in the perverted spirituality around you. That is a strong way to phrase it, but it is true. There is one way to the Father: through Christ Jesus. God is your Creator and Lord of the universe.

Block the New Age messages with His truth, praying or singing to God: *"He makes winds his messengers, flames of fire his servants. He set the earth on its foundations.... At [His] rebuke the waters fled... to the place [He] assigned for them."* (Psalm 104:4, 5a, 7a, 8b, NIV 1984)

"Who has gone up to heaven and come down? Who has gathered up the wind in the hollow of his hands? Who has wrapped up the waters in his cloak? Who has established all the ends of the earth? What is his name, and the name of his son? Tell me if you know!" (Proverbs 30:4, NIV 1984) Praise God!

19

Rescuing your Feet

Through prayer, God can repair any brokenness. You may not think of your feet or footwork as broken, but God does. He created them to be fully functioning for His glory, but they aren't. He has given you His word that He will rescue them.

Psalm 7:1, 2 (MSG)

GOD! GOD! I am running to you for dear life; the chase is wild. If they catch me, I'm finished.

Psalm 37:40 (MSG)

When we run to him, he saves us.

Psalm 40:1, 2 (MSG)

I waited and waited and waited for GOD. At last he looked; finally he listened. He lifted me out of the ditch, pulled me from deep mud. He stood me up on a solid rock to make sure I wouldn't slip.

Psalm 41:10 (MSG)

GOD, give grace, get me up on my feet.

Psalm 49:7 (MSG)

Really! There's no such thing as self-rescue, pulling yourself up by your bootstraps.

Psalm 56:12, 13 (MSG)

God, you did everything you promised, and I'm thanking you with all my heart. You pulled me from the brink of death, my feet from the cliff-edge of doom. Now I stroll at leisure with God in the sunlit fields of life.

Psalm 66:8, 9 (MSG)

Bless our GOD, O peoples! Give him a thunderous welcome! Didn't he set us on the road to life? Didn't he keep us out of the ditch?

Psalm 68:19 (MSG)

Blessed be the LORD – day after day he carries us along.

Psalm 70:1 (MSG)

GOD! Please hurry to my rescue! GOD, come quickly to my side!

Psalm 71:1, 2(MSG)

I run for dear life to GOD, I'll never live to regret it. Do what you do so well: get me out of this mess and up on my feet.

Psalm 86:17 (MSG)

Make a show of how much you love me so the bullies who hate me will stand there slack-jawed, As you, GOD, gently and powerfully put me back on my feet.

Psalm 91:9–12 (MSG)

Yes, because GOD's your refuge, the High God your very own home, Evil can't get close to you, harm can't get through the door. He ordered his angels to guard you wherever you go. If you stumble, they'll catch you; their job is to keep you from falling.

Psalm 103:6 (MSG)

GOD makes everything come out right; he puts victims back on their feet.

Psalm 116:7, 8 (MSG)

I said to myself, "Relax and rest. GOD has showered you with blessings. Soul, you've been rescued from death; Eye, you've been rescued from tears; And you, Foot, were kept from stumbling."

Psalm 119:25 (MSG)

I'm feeling terrible—I couldn't feel worse! Get me on my feet again. You promised, remember?

Psalm 138:2, 3 (MSG)

Thank you for your love, thank you for your faithfulness; Most holy is your name, most holy is your Word. The moment I called out, you stepped in; you made my life large with strength.

ENTERING: A call from God

"The hands and the feet of the Body of Christ have been amputated. It is time to reattach them," Rick Warren said to a small Christian audience in Toronto in 2007. His words are a stark picture of a dismembered body. What a dramatic call! But to whom? Only God is capable of putting His Body back together, of getting it back on its feet.

The Church is His body and Jesus Christ is the head. No matter what part you play, your role is to pray and act as He leads you. As you enter this devotion, examine the physical and the spiritual parallels of what your feet do in this world. Then as you walk with other Christ-followers, take the personal and corporate perspectives when asking God to rescue your feet.

All feet have three physical functions: stability, mobility, and the ability to bear weight. You can stand steadily, move readily, and carry more than your own body weight. Spiritually, the feet of the corporate body of Christ are believers, who carry the gospel message. This part of the body symbolizes the transforming change that God has wrought in the whole body. You stand in His power

- to hold you in God-fixed stability
- to move you in message mobility
- to carry the weight of His glory

The Hebrew word for "glory" also translates as "weight." Say a prayer using these words to affirm and describe God's holy purposes for your feet. His plan to rescue you is an eternal one; it began before you were born.

WALKING: A call-out to God

The Psalms teach us to call out to God. They model "deep calling to deep." In this long selection of verses you experience desperation, deliverance, and then declarations of God's great rescue. Read it through in a quiet prayerful voice. Think about your feet and how they function physically and spiritually. Pause often and let the Holy Spirit bring words and situations to mind. "Get me on my feet" is just one footwork metaphor that describes renewal or revival – physically or spiritually. Are there other footwork expressions that describe your needs? Use them as you call out to God to rescue you.

In your second reading, call out to God for others. Rearrange these exclamatory, exulting verses into a prayer. (See a sample at the end of this devotion.) You know people who need a physical and a spiritual rescue. Read your reorganization of these verses aloud in a stronger voice as many times as the Holy Spirit leads you, substituting names and phrases as you go.

In your third reading, hold the universal body of Christ in mind and heart as you call out to God for its rescue. There are parts of the body that need rescue desperately – from persecution, oppression, invasion, or apathy. Some parts of the body are in disarray because of how one part relates to the other: turning a cold shoulder, stepping on toes, or having a nose out of joint. Ask God to realign the whole body to the image of Christ. Now, think of your personal experience in the corporate body. Some members may have injured you, tainting your view of the whole. God knows the reconciliation and repair that is needed. Ask Him to bring healing to you and to the whole.

Before leaving this devotion, praise God that Jesus Christ took on a body and that by His Spirit, the body of Christ is present on earth. You have His fully functioning feet to follow. May your footwork bring glory to God.

FOLLOWING THROUGH: A call to action

Various organizations have unique ministries that rescue and revive feet around the world. Here are a few. Follow up with any that move you.

- Back on our feet.org – a running group for homeless people in various American cities
- God+Feet – an organization that created faith-inspired flip flops
- Agape House, Vancouver, B.C. – an opportunity for prostitutes in the downtown eastside to receive foot washing

- Society for Barefoot Living – a charity fighting foot disease in Ethiopia
- Soles4Souls – a charity that collects shoes for third world countries

Do you know of others?

A paraphrased prayer from the Psalms: Calling out to God to rescue your feet

God! God! I am running to you for dear life; the chase is wild. If they catch me, I'm finished (7:1, 2). God! Please hurry to my rescue! God, come quickly to my side (70:1). God, give grace, get me up on my feet (41:10). I run for dear life to God, I'll never live to regret it. Do what you do so well: get me out of this mess and up on my feet (71:1, 2). Make a show of how much you love me so the bullies who hate me will stand there slack-jawed, as you, God, gently and powerfully put me back on my feet (86:17). I'm feeling terrible—I couldn't feel worse! Get me on my feet again. You promised, remember (119:25)?

I waited and waited and waited for you. At last you looked; finally you listened. You lifted me out of the ditch, pulled me from deep mud. You stood me up on a solid rock to make sure I wouldn't slip (40:1, 2)?

When I run to you God, you save me (37:40). You did everything you promised, and I'm thanking you with all my heart. You pulled me from the brink of death, my feet from the cliff-edge of doom. Now I stroll at leisure with you in the sunlit fields of life (56:12, 13).

I bless you, God! I give you a thunderous welcome! Didn't you set me on the road to life? Didn't you keep me out of the ditch (66:8, 9)? Yes, because You are my refuge, You the High God my very own home, evil can't get close to me; harm can't get through the door. You ordered your angels to guard me wherever I go. If I stumble, they'll catch me; their job is to keep me from falling (91:9–12).

I said to myself, "Relax and rest. God has showered you with blessings. Soul, you've been rescued from death; Eye, you've been rescued from tears; and you, Foot, were kept from stumbling" (116:7, 8).

God, you make everything come out right; you put victims like me back on my feet (103:6). Blessed be you Lord – day after day you carry me along (68:19). Thank you for your love, thank you for your faithfulness; most holy is your name, most holy is your Word. The moment I called out, you stepped in; you made my life large with strength (138:2, 3). Really! There's no such thing as self-rescue, pulling yourself up by your bootstraps (49:7).

V

Direction on the Road –
Experiencing God's Leadership

20

Companions on the Road

Caution: walking with others is a test of care, comfort, and credibility. It is a two-way street; companions can influence each other positively and negatively.

Psalm 1:1 (NIV 1984)

Blessed is the man who does not walk in the counsel of the wicked or stand in the way of sinners or sit in the seat of mockers.

Psalm 41:9 (NKJV)

Even my own familiar friend in whom I trusted, Who ate my bread, Has lifted up his heel against me.
[This was quoted by Jesus in John 13:18 as Judas was identified as His betrayer.]

Proverbs 1:10, 15, 16 (MSG)

Dear friend, if bad companions tempt you, don't go along with them....

Oh, friend, don't give them a second look; don't listen to them for a minute. They're racing to a very bad end, hurrying to ruin everything they lay hands on.

Proverbs 2:20, 21 (MSG)

So – join the company of good men and women; keep your feet on the tried-and-true paths. It's the men who walk straight who will settle this land, the women with integrity who will last here.

Proverbs 3:27 (MSG)

Never walk away from someone who deserves help; your hand is God's hand for that person.

Jeremiah 38:22 (ESV)

Your trusted friends have deceived you and prevailed against you; now that your feet are sunk in the mud, they turn away from you.

Zechariah 8:23 (NLT)

Please let us walk with you, for we have heard that God is with you.

Amos 3:3 (NLT)

Can two people walk together without agreeing on the direction?

Philippians 3:16–19 (MSG)

Now that we're on the right track, let's stay on it. Stick with me, friends. Keep track of those you see running this same course, headed for this same goal. There are many out there taking other paths, choosing other goals, and trying to get you to go along with them. I've warned you of them many times; sadly, I'm having to do it again. All they want is easy street. They hate Christ's Cross. But easy street is a dead-end street.

2 Thessalonians 3:6 (ESV)

Now we command you, brothers, in the name of the Lord Jesus Christ, that you keep away from any brother who is walking in idleness and not in accord with the tradition that you received from us.

ENTERING: Check your feet

Think of all the people you spoke to or walked alongside yesterday. Every step you take, even in on-line relationships, is part of walking together. You know this for certain when relationships come apart. Feet and heart are stranded. You wonder where to go next.

Your companions can be family, friends, acquaintances, co-workers, heroes, or competitors. They are people who influence your behavior; they can affect your faith. Make two lists: "Companions I am grateful to walk with" and "Companions whose influence I am doubtful about." Ask God for deeper discernment as you move through this devotion.

Equally, you are an influence on the behavior and faith of others. Before you go on, confess that sometimes you walk in relationships with muddied feet and an injured heart. Pause for a minute with the Spirit of God and ask Him for cleansing – imagine a fountain of the Living Water to soak your feet in. Ask for His healing and renewal of your feet and heart so that your companions are blessed with the clear sense of Jesus in you.

WALKING: Decide what advice you need

Find the verse from Amos and circle it. Say it as a prayer to the Holy Spirit and ask Him to be your close companion as you move through these verses. Read the scriptures aloud in the voice of a loving friend. Do you notice any change in tone from verse to verse? Listen for the "do's and don'ts" of advice; for wisdom and warning. There's also insight into how badly some friendships end. Jesus knew this.

Reread the verses, stopping after each one. Rephrase them into your own words. Does the advice apply to you? Have you experienced something like this? How would you reorder the verses to reflect their importance to your life? What advice did God give you in this exercise?

Relationships, like footwork, fall into natural rhythms. You may not always pay attention to the direction you are going. Ponder for a few minutes where you are going with the people on your lists.

FOLLOWING THROUGH: Understand your influence

Circle the Zechariah verse. Does the Holy Spirit bring someone to mind for you to walk with? Or someone you should discontinue walking alongside?

Check your inventory of companions again and re-sort them according to these footwork dynamics:

- those you are following
- those who are following you
- those who follow Christ

Take a moment to ask God for wise friends, good leaders, forgiveness for those who have hurt or betrayed you, and the release of those who are hindering your walk with God.

Look up the words to the song "What a friend we have in Jesus."

21

Detours

It is a rare life that stays a steady course. God uses unexpected turns to challenge you. Your feet adapt to different terrain and to roundabout routes. You discover that you need Him along the way and that He has arranged every step you take.

Matthew 2:13–16; 19–23 (NLT)

After the wise men were gone, an angel of the LORD appeared to Joseph in a dream. "Get up! Flee to Egypt with the child and his mother," the angel said. "Stay there until I tell you to return, because Herod is going to search for the child to kill him."

That night Joseph left for Egypt with the child and Mary, his mother, and they stayed there until Herod's death. This fulfilled what the LORD had spoken through the prophet: "I called my Son out of Egypt."

Herod was furious when he realized that the wise men had outwitted him. He sent soldiers to kill all the boys in and around Bethlehem who were two years old and under, based on the wise men's report of the star's first appearance....

When Herod died, an angel of the LORD appeared in a dream to Joseph in Egypt. "Get up!" the angel said. "Take the child and his mother back to the land of Israel, because those who were trying to kill the child are dead."

So Joseph got up and returned to the land of Israel with Jesus and his mother. But when he learned that the new ruler of Judea was Herod's son Archelaus, he was afraid to go there. Then, after being warned in a dream, he left for the region of Galilee.

So the family went and lived in a town called Nazareth. This fulfilled what the prophets had said: "He will be called a Nazarene."

ENTERING: Diversion

Detours reroute us on the path to our destination. They can come up suddenly and mysteriously. The first step onto the detour is likely a conscious one – whether hesitant or confident; it is often a step of obedience.

Metaphors of feet inevitably merge with metaphors of the road or path; and merge again with metaphors of the map or the way. The wider your view, the more reduced the footwork seems. Think of a marathon – 26.2 miles of steps, perhaps not individually remembered apart from the one at the outset and the one at the finish line. Detours also offer the wide view of cumulative steps on a diverted path. The Bible offers examples of detours with deep meanings: Joseph's journey to Egypt, Israel's wandering in the desert, and the tribe of Judah's exile to Babylon. This devotion allows you to contemplate the detour Jesus and His family took as you gain insight into the unexpected turns you have taken. Focusing on the footwork helps you understand the motivation that prompts the feet to move.

I reflect on a summer evening when I was a teenager. My father lashed out and beat me when I came home from a movie date. My mother saw this as a clear sign for us to leave, an inevitable decision after suffering years of abuse. Within twenty-four hours, we fled to a city 2,000 miles across Canada. I was ready for adventure, so even in the midst of it I saw this detour from the bright side.

Your detours may not have been as dramatic – at least I hope not. But any sudden alteration of direction, any hidden corner can be jarring. You may not land on your feet at first. Before embarking on this study and prayer time, reflect on the diversions you have experienced. What alternate route did you find yourself on? Hold that memory in your heart throughout this time with God.

WALKING: Protection

God orchestrated a detour in the life of His Son. What does that say to you?

Ask the Holy Spirit to guide your reading of the verses. Go through twice, noticing the characters, their roles, and how they made decisions. What catches your attention? Do you get a sense of what is motivating them? And who is protecting them?

On your third reading, look at the details. Put yourself in Joseph's shoes; try to imagine his emotional and his physical responses to the commands of the angel, especially in light of the danger his family was in. Can you find the four footwork instructions Joseph received in his dream? Did he obey each one?

The footwork in this devotion is simple. Joseph got up and left. Later, Joseph got up and returned. Sometimes, the multiple steps we take in a "big move" get reduced or summarized into a single step. Imagine Mary and Joseph discussing how God led them supernaturally and what it was like to even make the first step. Once they were under way on the detour – or indeed, on their way back from the detour – they must have felt confident in God's protective leading.

Try to remember more details of that unexpected diversion in your life. Was there was a moment of recognition that your route had suddenly changed course? Can you remember what the first step was? If possible, describe your footwork before, during, and after the detour. What role did obedience or disobedience play? Did you sense that God was with you? Where have you ended up? (Check your feet; they always give a simple reading of location.)

Some detours are for life. No matter what causes them, they are part of God's plan. There is often a "Herod" and, thankfully more often, "wise men" redirecting you along new routes. Can you identify the players that God has used to orchestrate taking you to your unplanned destination? Ask God for what you need wherever you are along the path. If He prompts you to move along, be ready to obey. He has something in mind.

FOLLOWING THROUGH: Destination

I wonder if Jesus had childhood memories of Egypt or if He relived the time solely through His parents' recollections? Surely He admired their trust in following God's leading into unknown territory. It was all for their child's sake that they acted obediently. One day, he would return the favor.

Are your detour stories some of the more interesting ones that you tell? Did this passage help you reframe your own understanding of God diverting your path? Can you tell the story to a friend?

I am very glad that my detours didn't last a lifetime, though they nearly did. Shortly after my mother and I arrived in our new city, I heard the gospel story as if for the first time. I received Jesus into my heart. But, it was just a pit stop. For the next fourteen years, I pursued achievement and self-interest. My spiritual seeking went way off course. I didn't attend church and got caught back up in some New Age practices. I remember at one point realizing that I hadn't prayed in two years. God was at work but I couldn't see it. Later, I married, children arrived and we moved to a new country. These transitions led us to seek out a church community. God met us there and confirmed our faith in Him. We moved our household to yet another country where we started to study the bible in depth and with delight. The physical transitions were not the important detours; they paralleled the spiritual intersections and choices that opened up. After thirty-plus address changes in three different countries, I now live in the city I was born in. My feet and heart track deeply with God. I am certain He orchestrated every move to bring me full circle, as they say. To Him, as I say.

22

Guiding your feet

The guidance God gives your feet is foundational to all of life's decisions and directions. He wants you to ask Him for it.

Psalm 23:3 (NLT)

He renews my strength. He guides me along right paths, bringing honor to his name.

Psalm 32:8 (NLT)

The LORD says, "I will guide you along the best pathway for your life. I will advise you and watch over you."

Psalm 37:23, 24 (NLT)

The LORD directs the steps of the godly. He delights in every detail of their lives. Though they stumble, they will never fall, for the LORD holds them by the hand.

Psalm 119:105 (NLT)

Your word is a lamp to guide my feet and a light for my path.

Psalm 119:133 (NIV 1984)

Direct my footsteps according to your word; let no sin rule over me.

Psalm 139:23, 24 (MSG)

Investigate my life, O God, find out everything about me; Cross-examine and test me, get a clear picture of what I'm about; See for yourself whether I've done anything wrong— then guide me on the road to eternal life.

ENTERING: Focus on God

Challenging circumstances can immobilize you. When push comes to shove, your feet falter and you struggle to stand. As you recover your balance, your next step has your full attention. You seek advice on decisions to chart out the best way forward.

The right next step is to trust God. He is the prime mover and the One in whom you find your purpose. With His eternal view to your life, God is delighted to be your guide. You cannot see Him actually guide your feet. But you know that with Him, you can get up and out of whatever rut you are in. Open your hands and offer to God whatever challenge you need guidance with. Watch what He does with it through this devotion.

Pray that God would take your eyes off any confusion in you or around you. Ask for help in focusing your whole heart on trusting Him. Ask for His peace to really listen to His words. Acknowledge His all-seeing, all-knowing vantage point over your life. Ask Him for patience as you discover the way forward. Thank Him in advance for answered prayers. He is always delighted when you ask.

WALKING: Trust in God

When Jesus was pressed on all sides, He handled the pressure by being fully dependent on His Father. He didn't move until the Holy Spirit moved Him. He had heavenly guidance as He entered synagogues to teach, as He countered pompous arguments, and as He sought the lost and healed the lame. Every step of the way to the cross and beyond, Jesus modeled trust in God.

First, you want to understand how Jesus received assurance of heavenly guidance while He was on earth. Read the verses as a message from the Holy Spirit to Jesus. Then read and receive them as heaven's assurance to you. In Psalm 32, the Lord says "I will." Read the other verses and hear the Holy Spirit say "I will" to you. Do you hear His declarations that His word is trustworthy? The psalmist's voice gives God permission to examine your heart. In doing this, you can gauge your own trust in Him. Self-examination can uncover blocks. Trust, in turn, opens up the road God wants to take you on.

Next, with your own challenging circumstance in mind, go through this checklist. Ask for guidance and – where you can – express trust. I need / trust God to

- renew my strength
- guide me along right paths
- bring honor to His name
- guide me along the best pathway for my life
- advise me
- watch over me
- direct my steps
- delight in every detail of my life
- hold my hand so if I stumble, I won't fall
- guide me until I die
- provide His word as a lamp to guide my feet
- light my path
- direct my footsteps according to His word
- let no sin rule over me
- investigate my life
- find out everything about me
- cross-examine and test me
- get a clear picture of what I am about
- see what I have done wrong
- guide me on the road to eternal life

Put a tab or a bookmark on this page so that you can revisit this list. Try to gauge how God is increasing your trust in Him over time and through different challenges.

Following Through: Go to God

You can turn any of these expressions into one-line prayers:

- "Renew my strength."
- "Guide me along right paths."
- "Bring honor to Your name."
- "Guide me along the best pathway for my life."
- "Advise me."
- "Watch over me."
- "Direct my steps."

And so on.

Choose the ones that are most important to you and memorize them. Chances are you will need to go to God for guidance again soon.

23

Marches and Processions

Think of the messages that feet deliver: goose-stepping soldiers – taunting, the Million Man March – daunting. When God leads the march, His message is triumph – yours, in Christ.

Numbers 2:34 (NLT)

So the people of Israel did everything as the LORD had commanded Moses. Each clan and family set up camp and marched under their banners exactly as the LORD had instructed them.

2 Samuel 5:24 (NLT)

When you hear a sound like marching feet in the tops of the poplar trees, be on the alert! That will be the signal that the LORD is moving ahead of you to strike down the Philistine army.

Isaiah 42:13 (NIV 1984)

The LORD will march out like a mighty man, like a warrior he will stir up his zeal; with a shout he will raise the battle cry and will triumph over his enemies.

2 Corinthians 2:14 (NIV 1984)

But thanks be to God, who always leads us in triumphal procession in Christ and through us spreads everywhere the fragrance of the knowledge of him.

Hebrews 11:30 (NLT)

It was by faith that the people of Israel marched around Jericho for seven days, and the walls came crashing down. (See also Joshua 6:2–5.)

Revelation 3:5 (MSG)

Conquerors will march in the victory parade, their names indelible in the Book of Life. I'll lead them up and present them by name to my Father and his Angels

ENTERING: Marching in victory

In the 1960s someone famously but anonymously said, "We won when we started walking." The thousands who marched with Martin Luther King, Jr., to Montgomery, Alabama, sent the message that "normal" race relations in the American South were not tolerable. The marchers moved the dial on civil rights.

In 2012, in Calgary, Alberta, a March for Jesus spokesman, Nick Vujicic, is a man living without limbs. On the internet, in a strong, loving voice he called for others to "Be involved. Stand up against the gates of hell and redirect traffic."

Annually, Orthodox congregations across Ethiopia march with great pageantry to celebrate Jesus' baptism. Priests in dazzling robes carry their church's tabots, replicas of the Ark of the Covenant, to a central location where they stay overnight together. Millions of young and old, clothed in white, join the procession, covering the streets with fresh flowers and blessed grasses. On the way back to their respective churches, the priests chant as they carry the tabots. The faithful people march and dance to the drum beats and the rhythmic clink of sistrums.

Marches and processions are something to behold. Often they pronounce victory even before battle has taken place. Such is the case when you march with God, because the outcome of the battle has already been decided. The Holy Spirit is trying to get your attention. Look for Him at the front of the march as you begin this devotion.

WALKING: Leading from on high

Fall into step with the Holy Spirit. He is ready for you to follow. Read the verses through once; stop after each one to visualize the scene.

- In Numbers 2, can you see the banners?
- In 2 Samuel, can you hear the sound around the tops of the trees?
- In 2 Corinthians, can you smell the fragrance?
- In Hebrews, can you feel the ground shake?

Do you wish you could step into the action of a particular verse? What attracts you?

On second reading, grab your pen. Circle those marching in the procession and double underline who is leading. In the margin beside the verse, note another detail about God and His leadership that seems important to you. At the end of the verses, compile your image of God.

Finally contemplate the verse from 2 Corinthians, as parsed below:

- thanking God
- following His triumphal procession
- identifying with Christ
- spreading everywhere the fragrance of victory that
- knowing Him brings

How did God train Israel to do these things? How is He training you? What intrigues you about leaving a fragrance of Christ in your wake?

FOLLOWING THROUGH: Imagining more

When two walk together, their footwork naturally coordinates to a similar pace, length of stride and rhythm. Multiply that by hundreds, thousands. Imagine the picture and the impact each pair of feet make.

Research has proven that regular, heavy footfalls on crowded dance floors are a source of energy, enough to provide the electricity for the dance clubs themselves. Imagine the energy generated by the coordinated impact of feet on the ground in marches and processions. Imagine, spiritually, that those yoked with Christ harness the energy of God through His Spirit in each one. That is the Body of Christ on the move.

The message these feet deliver is _____
(You fill in the blank.)

24

The Road to Emmaus

Emotions can affect your awareness of what is happening around you. On the road to Emmaus, two downcast disciples were so focused on a past experience that they barely noticed their feet moving forward. In this devotion, you reflect on what is preventing you from seeing Jesus in your spiritual walk.

Luke 24:13–32 (NIV)

Now that same day, two of them were going to a village called Emmaus, about seven miles from Jerusalem. They were talking with each other about everything that had happened. As they talked and discussed these things with each other, Jesus himself came up and walked with them; but they were kept from recognizing him. He asked them, "What are you discussing together as you walk along?"

They stood still, their faces downcast. One of them, named Cleopas, asked him, "Are you to the only one visiting Jerusalem who does not know the things that have happened here in these days?" "What things?" he asked.

"About Jesus of Nazareth," they replied. "He was the prophet, powerful in word and deed before God and all the people. The chief priests and our rulers handed him over to be sentenced to death, and they crucified him; but we had hoped that he was the one who was going to redeem Israel. And what is more, it is the third day since all this took place. In addition,

some of our women amazed us. They went to the tomb early this morning but didn't find his body. They came and told us that they had seen a vision of angels, who said just as the women had said, but him they did not see.

He said to them, "How foolish are you, and how slow to believe all that the prophets have spoken! Did not the Messiah have to suffer these things and then enter his glory?" And beginning with Moses and all the Prophets, he explained to them what was said in all the scriptures concerning himself.

As they approached the village to which they were going, Jesus continued on as if he were going farther. But they urged him strongly, "Stay with us, for it is nearly evening; the day is almost over." So he went in to stay with them.

When he was at the table with them, he took bread, gave thanks, broke it and began to give it to them. Then their eyes opened and they recognized him, and he disappeared from their sight. They asked each other "Were not our hearts burning within us while he talked with us on the road and opened the Scriptures to us?"

ENTERING: Turning point

A fork in the road is an apt metaphor for the spiritual challenge the two ordinary disciples faced as they walked along. They could go down the road of commiserating their loss of a rabbi. Or they could console each other that the fulfillment of the scriptural prophecies pointing to the sacrifice of God's Son was their gain. Jesus presented them with this choice face to face. Their Savior demonstrated the newness of life that His resurrection had won for them. *"This is the way, walk in it."* (Isaiah 30:21, NIV)

Ask the Holy Spirit for alertness, for eyes to see and ears to hear His revelations in these verses. While this account is a rich reservoir for metaphor, it is not a parable. It really happened. Ask God to use this road story to transform the way you walk and talk with Jesus and to help you choose the right fork – moving from an ordinary to an extraordinary walk.

WALKING: Taking turns

These verses could be a script for a short film. There is a beginning, middle, and end – and a lot of action. Pretend that you are the director. No pressure! Read through once before you begin the work of motivating and directing your actors. Let your mind roam as you begin to picture the location and the length of the film. Get ready to go over the script with the three main actors.

On their first reading your goal is to coordinate movement. Ask the actors to pay attention to all the activity. For example, as the disciples walk, they take turns talking about the painful loss of their teacher. Jesus joins them on the road and enters their conversation. Get your actors thinking about the naturalness of the scene by saying, "The rhythms of walking and talking resemble the rhythms of life." Ask them to make some notes on their scripts: underlining the motions (walking or stopping) and using different colors to highlight the words of the speakers.

On the second reading, your goal is to give the actors deeper motivation and compassion for the characters they will play. Give them three "why" questions:

- Why were the disciples kept from recognizing Jesus initially?
- Why did Jesus act as if He were going further down the road?
- Why did they finally recognize Jesus?

Ask the actors to picture themselves on the road. Give them some quiet time to contemplate these questions. What kind of deep thoughts and discussion did these questions generate?

On the final reading for today, you want your actors to understand that the disciples had a supernatural encounter on the road that changed their lives forever. At the outset, the two were downcast. Then they experienced a kind of ecstasy that they felt as spiritual heartburn. Finally, they witnessed a miracle. How do you coach your actors on the facial expressions and gestures reflecting these inward changes?

Tell them that their homework is to read to the end of the chapter to see how the disciples' footwork changed after their encounter with Jesus.

FOLLOWING THROUGH: Turning inward

As the director, you take the script home so you can mull it over. The Holy Spirit wants to carry on an inner conversation. You can't get some parts of the story out of your mind.

- The disciples didn't recognize Jesus even though they were face to face.
- Jesus chastened the disciples for being foolish and slow of heart for not believing what the prophets had spoken.

The Holy Spirit isn't letting go. Even as director, you need coaching to see the forks in the road you have faced personally. These are challenges to the direction of your faith:

- Do you see Jesus walking with you?
- If not, what is preventing you from seeing him?

25

Road Signs

Signs direct us to destinations and warn of hazards or changes in road conditions. What is true in the material world is true in the spiritual. God's signs give us a sense of the spiritual conditions of the road ahead of us.

Psalm 19:7, 8, 11 (MSG)

The revelation of God is whole and pulls our lives together. The signposts of God are clear and point out the right road. The life-maps of God are right, showing the way to joy. The directions of God are plain and easy on the eyes.... There's more: God's Word warns us of danger and directs us to hidden treasure. Otherwise how will we find our way?

Psalm 25:10 (MSG)

From now on every road you travel will take you to GOD. Follow the Covenant signs; Read the charted directions.

Psalm 119:9–12 (MSG)

How can a young person live a clean life?

By carefully reading the map of your Word. I'm single-minded in pursuit of you; don't let me miss the road signs you've posted. I've banked your promises in the vault of my heart so I won't sin myself bankrupt. Be blessed, GOD; train me in your ways of wise living.

Psalm 119:29–32 (MSG)

Barricade the road that goes Nowhere; grace me with your clear revelation. I choose the true road to Somewhere, I post your road signs at every curve and corner. I grasp and cling to whatever you tell me; GOD, don't let me down! I'll run the course you lay out for me if you'll just show me how.

Proverbs 4:11, 12, 14, 15 (MSG)

I'm writing out clear directions to Wisdom Way, I'm drawing a map to Righteous Road. I don't want you ending up in blind alleys, or wasting time making wrong turns.... Don't take Wicked Bypass, don't so much as set foot on that road. Stay clear of it; give it a wide berth. Make a detour and be on your way.

Proverbs 4:25–27 (MSG)

Keep your eyes straight ahead; ignore all sideshow distractions. Watch your step, and the road will stretch out smooth before you. Look neither right nor left; leave evil in the dust.

Proverbs 16:17 (MSG)

The road of right living bypasses evil; watch your step and save your life.

Isaiah 26:8 (MSG)

We're in no hurry, GOD. We're content to linger in the path sign-posted with your decisions. Who you are and what you've done are all we'll ever want.

ENTERING: Sign language

In scripture, God's signs were critical to the junctures of life for His chosen people. The rainbow after the flood was God's sign, a promise to Noah never to submerge the earth again. The small cloud in the sky during the drought told Elijah that God was faithfully answering his prayer for rain. Mary's virgin conception was a sign of a Savior to be born. The destruction of the Temple after Jesus' death was a sign that God's presence was no longer there. The Bible's symbolism allows us to contemplate the supernatural in simple ways. Signs reduce the distance between God and His people. They assure you and me of His unseen presence on life's journey.

Taking the figurative meaning of signs to a pedestrian level, current-day followers of Jesus look for signs on the road of life. You need warnings and guidance over the uneven ground of your circumstances. Proverbs 11:14 says you can lose your way without good direction. Road signs, both physical and spiritual, command your attention (Assuming you are on a road and not in the wilderness that is!)

As you enter this devotion, take a moment to stand still in God's presence. Look around. Describe where you are physically and spiritually. Are you at a crossroads in your job or relationships? What kind of road are you on? Is it the one you want to be on? Where have you come from and where do you want to go?

WALKING: One way – "Enter"

On your first reading, ask God to show you the sign in each verse. Look for signs that indicate

- a bypass
- danger
- a dead end
- a detour
- do not turn
- a new direction
- speed slowing

- a warning
- a wrong turn

As you go over each verse again, ask God if that sign is meant for you. Did you notice the sign for blind alleys and hidden treasure? This is no ordinary road! Do you feel warned and hesitant about moving forward, or just the opposite: inspired and ready to go? Use your gut feelings to help you. Why? God gave you adrenalin, pain, and other signs inside your body that you can read as well.

On your next turn through the verses, underline the commands. They begin with a verb and imply "you" as a subject. Take them seriously. They come from our Father in heaven. See how many you can find. How do commands relate to signs? Consider this physically and spiritually.

Finally, circle the most meaningful verse to you. Put a date beside it and note what the sign warns you of, directs you to, or informs you of. Are you ready to move on and discover what lies ahead?

FOLLOWING THROUGH: Crosswalk ahead

God wants us to read the signs He posts. He also enlists us in His "making sense of the road" project. Put up your own signs, as you see Him. Tell others how to get to Him. These signs, like testimonies, tell people where you have been and what God did there. *"Set up road signs; put up guideposts. Mark well the path by which you came."* (Jeremiah 31:21a, NLT)

What signs would you put up for your friends? For your family?

26

Wise Moves

As you go through life, you accumulate wisdom. Sometimes, you need fresh wisdom. Other times you need to reassess what you have before you go forward.

Proverbs 1:7 (MSG)

Start with GOD—the first step in learning is bowing down to GOD; only fools thumb their noses at such wisdom and learning.

Proverbs 3:27 (MSG)

Never walk away from someone who deserves help; your hand is God's hand for that person.

Proverbs 4:6 (NLT)

Don't turn your back on wisdom, for she will protect you. Love her, and she will guard you.

Proverbs 4:26, 27 (NLT)

Mark out a straight path for your feet; stay on the safe path. Don't get side-tracked; keep your feet from following evil.

Proverbs 6:20, 22a (NLT)

My son, obey your father's commands, and don't neglect your mother's instruction.... When you walk, their counsel will lead you.

Proverbs 13:20 (NLT)

Walk with the wise and become wise; associate with fools and get in trouble.

Proverbs 15:21b (ESV)

A man of understanding walks straight ahead.

Proverbs 25:17 (NKJV)

Seldom set foot in your neighbor's house, Lest he become weary of you and hate you.

Proverbs 28:26 (NIV 1984)

He who trusts in himself is a fool, but he who walks in wisdom is kept safe.

Jeremiah 10:23 (NIV 1984)

I know, O LORD, that a man's life is not his own; it is not for man to direct his steps.

Hosea 14:9 (NIV 1984)

Who is wise? He will realize these things. Who is discerning? He will understand them. The ways of the LORD are right; the righteous walk in them, but the rebellious stumble in them.

Ephesians 5:15, 16 (ESV)

Look carefully then how you walk, not as unwise but as wise, making the best use of the time, because the days are evil.

ENTERING: Getting God's perspective

Sometimes life is a maze. The pathway of unseen twists and turns is a picture of opposition, unclear choices and confusion. Limited vision, corners, and possible dead ends obstruct or divert you. Every move counts.

When your life choices are complex, next steps need to be intentional. Wisdom will help you decide how to move. In Jesus, you get an overview of the maze of your life. He has the perspective of God's will and plans for your life. A wise move – directed by His Spirit – brings your next move into alignment with God's will.

Think for a moment about where you are today. What was your most recent decision – whether in relationships, work, or home? Were there any unexpected turns, blocked routes, or time wasted worrying? Did you seek God's wisdom before you moved? Ask Him to show you how wisdom affects your walk in His will.

WALKING: Skirting the dangers

Wisdom is rarely learned in one place, at one time. This devotion represents "gathered wisdom" for the way forward. Read the scriptures once. As you do, notice any familiar-sounding verses – not exact words perhaps, but the gist. For example, look at Proverbs 13:20. Has anyone suggested you "choose your friends wisely"? Do other verses resonate in that way? Are any pertinent to your current decisions of where to go next?

Go through the verses again. Most are framed as advice. Think of each one as part of a dialogue: the verse is the answer, you supply the question. The television game-show Jeopardy has an answer-question format. You receive an answer and then respond with the appropriate question. For example, to Proverbs 4:6, you might ask, "Why shouldn't I turn my back on wisdom?" or "Why should I care about wisdom?" To Psalm 15:21b, "How does a man of understanding walk?" Or "What do I need to understand?"

As you walk through the verses a final time, picture the Holy Spirit instructing and cautioning in a range of situations you face. Identify the verse which gives you wisdom about

- planning a future move
- thinking when you walk
- submitting every step to God
- walking safely
- learning while you walk with others
- taking other avenues
- making wrong turns
- walking alongside those who need help
- giving the whole route to God
- moving away from God
- knowing your destination
- walking intentionally
- limiting your footwork
- walking in God's ways

What kind of wisdom do you need for your next move? Copy out the verse that will prompt a wise move.

FOLLOWING THROUGH: Sketching a plan

Think back to the maze comparison.

A maze is not easy to draw but you may be able to manage a rough sketch. At the very least, close your eyes and picture yourself inside a maze of hedges. Let the route represent the challenges or decisions you are currently facing. It is difficult to see your way ahead. One wrong move and you may waste time. Two wrong moves and…

Ask the Holy Spirit to direct your steps and to use this drawing as a tool to help you. Remember that your footwork, not your artwork, indicate obedience to Him.

Title your drawing "My Wise Moves." Write Proverbs 1:7 at the beginning of the maze. Let the opposite end of the drawing represent your goal: obedience to God's will. Thoughtfully, anticipate the challenging decisions you may face. Label your drawing accordingly. Do any of the verses from this devotion help you bypass these challenges? Write them in. Continue consulting with the Holy Spirit every time you are faced with a choice. Yielding to Him will enable you to walk in wisdom all the way to the goal.

At a later time, go back to your drawing and update it. What was God's design in helping you make wise moves? Can you see it from His perspective now?

VII

Distractions and Obstructions
– *Avoiding the Pitfalls*

27

Entrapment

Be alert to the ground game in spiritual conflict. Be aware that God goes on the offence when your feet are trapped.

Psalm 40:1, 2 (NIV)

I waited patiently for the LORD; he turned to me and heard my cry. He lifted me out of the slimy pit, out of the mud and mire; he set my feet on a rock and gave me a firm place to stand.

Psalm 91:2, 3 (NLT)

This I declare about the LORD: He alone is my refuge, my place of safety; he is my God, and I trust him. For he will rescue you from every trap.

Psalm 140:4, 5 (NKJV)

Keep me, O LORD, from the hands of the wicked; Preserve me from violent men Who have purposed to make my steps stumble. The proud have hidden a snare for me, and cords; They have spread a trap by the wayside; They have set traps for me.

Psalm 142:3 (NLT)

When I am overwhelmed, you alone know the way I should turn. Wherever I turn, my enemies have set traps for me.

Jeremiah 5:26 (NIV)

"Among my people are the wicked who lie in wait like men who snare birds and like those who set traps to catch people."

Deuteronomy 32:35 (NLT)

I [the Lord] will take revenge; I will pay them back. In due time their feet will slip. Their day of disaster will arrive, and their destiny will overtake them.

Job 18:5, 8–11 (NIV)

"The lamp of a wicked man is snuffed out; the flame of his fire stops burning.... His feet thrust him into a net; he wanders into its mesh. A trap seizes him by the heel; a snare holds him fast. A noose is hidden for him on the ground; a trap lies in his path. Terrors startle him on every side and dog his every step."

Jeremiah 18:22 (NIV)

Let a cry be heard from their houses when you suddenly bring invaders against them, for they have dug a pit to capture me and have hidden snares for my feet.

ENTERING: Vulnerable feet

Thanks to the new normal of 24/7 cable news and graphic movies, you are familiar with war zones. Sadly, you know that soldiers on foot patrol are vulnerable to land mines and improvised explosive devices (IEDs). Feet are literally at risk. War vets who learn to walk again on prosthetic limbs are inspiring. Foot injuries or losses demonstrate how vital feet are. Have you thought much about this?

Even though you cannot see spiritual warfare, you walk through a battlefield every day. Military metaphors such as strategies, tactics, and weaponry help you picture spiritual conflict. They also help you pray. As a foot soldier or follower of Christ, your feet are open to attack. Genesis 3:15 explains why feet are targets and what comes of the enemy's target practice. In Psalm 110:1 we see Jesus' feet resting on the footstool of His enemies, military victory in hand.

Entrapment is the enemy's tactic to immobilize you physically, emotionally, and spiritually. In these verses, you will read various descriptions of attacks on feet and faith. You need to be aware of Satan's devices so that he does not take advantage of you (2 Corinthians 2:11). Think back on your past couple of days. Did you walk through any emotional minefields that threatened to blow up? Have you felt stuck in one place for too long? Spiritually, you don't just get to witness the battle going on between good and evil; you have to walk through it.

Bow your head now and speak aloud your honor and trust of God's sovereignty. He is mightier than anything or anyone trying to trap you.

WALKING: Mighty God

Read through the verses once, noticing the interplay among God, the enemy, and believers. There is a lot of conflict around your feet. Even though you are often under attack, God always offers His help. Find the verse that you think best encapsulates this. Ask the Holy Spirit to trigger a memory of an experience that has seemed like an insurmountable trap. Hold it in mind.

On second reading, ask God to change your thinking about traps the enemy may be setting even now. To get this perspective, you will take these verses apart.

On an empty page, draw three columns with the following headings:

- The enemy tries to immobilize my feet
- God's response to my entrapments
- God's response to the enemy's activity

Using the verses, fill in the blanks and add more:

1. The enemy tries to immobilize my feet:
- in a slimy pit, in ____ and _____, in a trap.
- in the hands of the _____.
- violent men make me _____.
- the _____ have _____ a snare for me.
- cords are spread like a _____.
- everywhere I turn there are _____, the snares of _____.

2. God's response to my entrapments:
- He _____ to me and _____ my cry, _____ me out of the slimy pit, set my _____ on a rock, gave me a firm place to stand.
- He is my _____.
- He _____ me.
- He knows the ____ I should turn.
- He gives me _____.

3. God's response to the enemy's activity:
- He takes _____.
- He pays them _____.
- He brings _____ against them.
- He makes their _____ slip.
- He thrusts their feet into a ____.
- He sets a trap to seize him by the _____.

Find the verses that advise what you should do in midst of all this conflict:

- Wait patiently for the Lord.
- Declare who the Lord is and what He can and will do.
- Trust Him.
- Turn to Him when you are overwhelmed.

Notice how much God does and relatively, how little is expected of you?

FOLLOWING THROUGH: Empowered prayer

These verses on entrapment clearly picture God's victory over the enemy. They also give you words to use in prayer. Prayer is that communication with God that bursts forth from a happy or a hurting heart. Whether you are caught in the middle of a trap or have just been sprung, these verses direct you how to take God at His word.

Earlier you asked the Holy Spirit to trigger a memory of an insurmountable trap you experienced or may now be held in. Using the phrases of what to do in the midst of conflict, ask God for the courage and strength to do each one. Name them. Now, praise God using the words that describe His response to your situation, even if you can't see it or feel it. Praise Him on faith. Now, using the words that describe God's response to the enemy's trap in your life, declare, in faith, what God is doing and will do. Jesus has already freed you from the fetters.

28

Following other gods

God warns wayward feet that follow other gods. This wrong move has big consequences.

Exodus 20:3 (NLT)

You must not have any other god but me.

Deuteronomy 28:14 (NIV 1984)

Do not turn aside from any of the commands I give you today, to the right or to the left, following other gods and serving them.

Deuteronomy 29:18 (NLT)

I am making this covenant with you so that no one among you—no man, woman, clan, or tribe—will turn away from the LORD our God to worship these gods of other nations, and so that no root among you bears bitter and poisonous fruit.

Psalm 115:3, 4, 7, 8 (NKJV)

But our God is in heaven; He does whatever He pleases. Their idols are silver and gold, The work of men's hands…. They have hands but do not handle; Feet they have, but do not walk; Nor do they mutter through their throat. Those who make them are like them; So is everyone who trusts in them.

Jeremiah 16:11b–13a (NKJV)

"They have walked after other gods and have served them and worshiped them, and have forsaken Me and not kept My law. And you have done worse than your fathers, for behold, each one follows the dictates of his own evil heart, so that no one listens to Me. Therefore, I will cast you out of the land."

Jeremiah 18:15–17 (NLT)

But my people are not so reliable, for they have deserted me; they burn incense to worthless idols. They have stumbled off the ancient highways and walk in muddy paths. Therefore, their land will become desolate, a monument to their stupidity. All who pass by will be astonished and will shake their heads in amazement. I will scatter my people before their enemies as the east wind scatters dust. And in all their trouble I will turn my back on them and refuse to notice their distress.

Ezekiel 14:3 (NKJV)

These men have set up their idols in their hearts, and put before them that which causes them to stumble into iniquity.

Micah 4:5 (NLT)

Though the nations around us follow their idols, we will follow the LORD our God forever and ever.

1 Corinthians 10:14 (NLT)

So, my dear friends, flee from the worship of idols.

2 Corinthians 4:4 (NIV 1984)

The god of this age has blinded the minds of unbelievers, so that they cannot see the light of the gospel of the glory of Christ, who is the image of God.

Philippians 3:18, 19 (ESV)

For many, of whom I have often told you and now tell you even with tears, walk as enemies of the cross of Christ. Their end is destruction, their god is their belly, and they glory in their shame with minds set on earthly things.

ENTERING: Identifying a counterfeit

You have probably noticed a proliferation of counterfeit goods. Purses, watches, and even artwork are copied from original designs, with varying degrees of success. Imitation happens in the spiritual realm, too. Counterfeiting truth began the moment people turned from God to listen to the alluring advice of a snake.

How do you know if you have been following other gods? You may think, "Who me? There are no golden calves in my life." Or are there? Worshiping the golden calf was a historical act in the book of Exodus, but it has a wider meaning now. It represents anything – tangible or not – that you inordinately revere. Career goals, financial security, or even your children's achievements can overly preoccupy you. You may have good and socially acceptable priorities, but when they compete with God, they are your idols. By checking your heart, you can discover who or what is at the center of it. Who have you been following? Feet always leave a trail.

Ask the Holy Spirit, who gives discernment, to assist you with every reflection in this devotion.

WALKING: Seeing where the parallels end

Read through all the verses. Note the various footwork expressions: turn aside, stumble, flee, and others. Ask the Holy Spirit to help you examine this topic and your heart.

Following other gods is like a "parallel universe" to following the one true God. What you worship shapes both your conduct and your character. Before you begin comparisons, put a big star beside God's commandment in Exodus. The commands to your feet are coming; this is just the bold, blunt ban from God Himself. Next, note the parallel spiritual tracks of worship in Micah. See the difference? Does this parallelism concern you? Do you see it and condone it in daily life? Should God just tolerate it?

Ask the Holy Spirit to show you how the counterfeiting is happening.

- In black, circle the word "root" in Deuteronomy 29.
- With close reading of all verses, use black again to underline people's actions toward other gods. Also use black to underline what their feet are doing.
- In blue, circle the word "fruit" in Deuteronomy 29. (Note the relationship between "root" and "fruit").
- In the same blue, underline any commands and consequences that God issues to those who follow other gods.

In the 2 Corinthians verse, we get an explanation of how people have been taken in by counterfeits. The chapter "Walking in Darkness" paints a picture of just how impaired our judgment is.

Is there any area in your life in which you feel you have shown impaired judgment recently? Are there any things, people or ideals you have been worshipping in your life? Confess this to God, and ask him to help you stop idolizing false gods.

FOLLOWING THROUGH: Following the One and only

Our God is a jealous God. He loves you very much. He doesn't want your attention diverted from following Him.

On a piece of paper, list the various idols that have at one time or another captivated you. Go on, fill the page. If you identified a false god currently in your life, add that to the bottom of the list in capitals. Take a moment to reflect on where you would be now if you had followed any one of those fake gods on the trajectory you were headed. Breathe a deep prayerful, thankful sigh of relief. Out loud, acknowledge what Jesus did for you on the cross, what it means to be reconciled with your Heavenly Father, and what great things the Spirit of God leads you into.

Now, rip the paper up. It is garbage. Those things were nothing compared to the glory of the one true God. True.

29

Footholds

Have you ever heard the expression "Don't let the enemy get a foothold"? If you are a follower of Jesus, then God's work is to secure His foothold in your life.

Part One:

Psalm 69:2a, 14b (ESV)

I sink in deep mire, where there is no foothold...Let me be delivered from my enemies and from the deep waters.

Psalm 36:11a (NKJV)

Let not the foot of pride come against me.

Psalm 73:2, 3 (NIV 1984)

But as for me, my feet had almost slipped; I had nearly lost my foothold. For, I envied the arrogant when I saw the prosperity of the wicked.

Psalm 106:36 (NKJV)

They served their idols, which became a snare to them.

Isaiah 47:10 (NLT)

"You felt secure in your wickedness. 'No one sees me,' you said. But your 'wisdom' and 'knowledge' have led you astray, and you said, "I am the only one, and there is no other."

Jeremiah 18:12b (NKJV)

"So we will walk according to our own plans, and we will every one obey the dictates of his evil heart."

Daniel 4:37b (ESV)

I ... praise and extol and honor the King of heaven, for his works are right and his ways are just; and those who walk in pride he is able to humble.

Ephesians 4:26, 27 (NIV 1984)

"In your anger do not sin." Do not let the sun go down while you are still angry, and do not give the devil a foothold.

Colossians 3:5–7 (NIV 1984)

Put to death, therefore, whatever belongs to your earthly nature: sexual immorality, impurity, lust, evil desires and greed, which is idolatry. Because of these, the wrath of God is coming. You used to walk in these ways, in the life you once lived.

1 Timothy 6:9b, 10 (MSG)

Lust for money brings trouble and nothing but trouble. Going down that path, some lose their footing in the faith completely and live to regret it bitterly ever after.

Part Two:

1 Peter 5:6–9 (NIV 1984)

Humble yourselves, therefore, under God's mighty hand, that he may lift you up in due time. Cast all your anxiety on him because he cares for you. Be self-controlled and alert. Your enemy the devil prowls around like a roaring lion looking for someone to devour. Resist him, standing firm in the faith, because you know that your brothers throughout the world are undergoing the same kind of sufferings.

Ephesians 6:10–12 (NLT)

A final word: Be strong in the LORD and in his mighty power. Put on all of God's armor so that you will be able to stand firm against all strategies of the devil. For, we are not fighting against flesh-and-blood enemies, but against evil rulers and authorities of the unseen world, against mighty powers in this dark world, and against evil spirits in the heavenly places.

ENTERING: Toehold, then foothold

A mountain climber's foot searches for a toehold on a rock face and then grips further to secure a foothold. A military unit captures territory from its enemy and uses that foothold as a base from which to resupply. Both mountain climbers and military captains treat the foothold as a temporary place of advantage in order to move forward and cover more ground. Spiritually, the Kingdom of God has a foothold in the life of every believer, advancing God's reign as you walk by faith. Interestingly, the word "foothold" is also strongly associated with the enemy of God, to describe the shackles he uses and the places he covets in your life.

This devotion helps you pay attention to the footholds the enemy wants to establish and what you can do about it. Where Satan has already gained a foothold, God's military purpose is to remove and regain the territory through prayer. When you pray you give God a footing on the contested ground of your heart. Your surrender to God is His advantage in the battle. Your obedience to following God's ways hastens the enemy's retreat.

The enemy is always active, looking for spiritual footholds in all of our lives. His goal is to open the way for further destruction. This false ally had no hold on Christ Jesus because Jesus loved the Father and obeyed Him (John 14:30, 31). Jesus' straightforward strategy should be yours as well.

As you enter the time of devotion, ask the Holy Spirit to put your inner spirit on high alert so you can listen well.

WALKING: Ten footholds, ten commands

Read through Part One of the verses to find examples of enemy footholds. Notice what happens to your feet along the way. There are, of course, more than ten footholds that the enemy is capable of establishing in your life. These verses just get you started.

Now walk through the verses with your heart focused on the good and secure things God wants for you. Write the opposite, godly foothold beside each enemy foothold listed in the passages. God's coveted footholds are

- humility
- godly desire
- contentment
- worship of God
- God's wisdom and knowledge
- peace
- the mind of Christ
- belief or faith

- rest in God
- sexual purity

Ask the Holy Spirit to point out any footholds that the enemy has in your life these days. Surrender and ask God take His advantage so that He can advance His purposes for you.

Read Part Two of the verses and underline the commands. (Clue: Commands always start with a verb and imply the subject "you.") The 1 Peter verse says, "Cast your anxiety on Him because He cares for you." Again, like Jesus' defense against any enemy incursion, it is a simple strategy. Obeying this and other commands allows God to place His foothold in your life.

FOLLOWING THROUGH: Foothold prayers

There are likely footholds of enemy activity in your life. The minute you criticize another person, pride takes its position. One wish that you had what another person has, and envy is in action. If you despair over the enemy's influence in your life, you have given him too much credence and built a little altar of attention for him. Be careful, for he is a cunning counterfeiter. He wants what is rightfully God's.

In your quiet time, enlist the Holy Spirit to help you examine your wandering heart and look for waywardness in your feet as well. God wants us focused on Jesus (Hebrews 12:2), believing that while we cannot see all that is happening (2 Corinthians 4:17, 18) the Lord Almighty has it all in hand. Pray about your footing. Give God the advantage in the next step you take.

30

Self-inflicted Traps

Feet and footwork are good indicators of how your life is going. If you walk freely and safely, that's wonderful. There are metaphors that describe the opposite: traps, snares, ambushes, and pits. Some of these are of your own making.

Job 18:5–10 (NKJV)

"The light of the wicked indeed goes out, and the flame of his fire does not shine. The light is dark in his tent, and his lamp beside him is put out. The steps of his strength are shortened, and his own counsel casts him down. For, he is cast into a net by his own feet, and he walks into a snare. The net takes him by the heel, and a snare lays hold of him. A noose is hidden for him on the ground and a trap for him in the road.

Proverbs 1:15–19 (NLT)

My child, don't go along with them! Stay away from their paths. They rush to commit evil deeds. They hurry to commit murder. If a bird sees a trap being set, it knows to stay away. But these people set an ambush for themselves; they are trying to set themselves killed. Such is the fate of all who are greedy for money; it robs them of life.

Proverbs 22:5 (NIV)

In the paths of the wicked are snares and pitfalls, but those who would preserve their life stay far from them.

Proverbs 28:10 (NLT)

Those who lead good people along an evil path will fall into their own trap.

Proverbs 29:25 (NIV 1984)

Fear of man will prove to be a snare, but whoever trusts in the LORD is kept safe.

Psalm 9:15 (NKJV)

The nations have sunk down in the pit which they made; in the net which they hid, their own foot is caught.

Psalm 141:10 (NIV 1984)

Let the wicked fall into their own nets, while I pass by in safety.

Hebrews 12:1b-2a (NIV)

Let us throw off everything that hinders and the sin that so easily entangles. And let us run with perseverance the race marked out for us, fixing our eyes on Jesus, the pioneer and perfecter of faith.

ENTERING: I'm stuck. Help!

Self-inflicted traps don't garner much sympathy. For me, getting caught ultimately brings a return to tracking with God. Where would I be without His rescue? Having enough company in my crimes used to reinforce the lie that stumbling on dark roads was the way to walk through life. Immoral sexual behavior, substance abuse, theft, dissension, following other gods, coveting, jealousy and other gritty God-dishonoring choices over the years put me into positions that I couldn't easily reverse out of. Once I was stuck, I learned to cry out to God for help. You may not relate to these sins; we all have our own lists. In any case, self-inflicted traps are common to us all.

Imagine that you have fallen into a damp, dark pit (without your cell phone) and landed in such a way that your legs and feet are injured. Poor you! What's your first option? Look up and call for help. While you are waiting for help to come, you have ample time to reflect on how you landed there in the first place. God is in the rescue business. Being merciful means He doesn't discriminate based on who or what caused your descent. He just wants you back, and He will make you whole again. It is a very good deal. When you find yourself in shackles of your own making or a pit you dug for yourself, the first thing you need to do is look up and call upon God for help.

WALKING: I can't get out on my own.

Read through the scriptures once. Most of the verses are short and probably uncomfortable. You may wonder whether they even apply to you. To make them more provocative and, hopefully, more effective, think of them as mirrors to see yourself in. Ask the Holy Spirit to hold them up as you walk through again. Get His help with some of the words you may want to skim over – such as "wicked" and "evil."

Check the Bible for what Jesus says about "anger" and "murder" in Matthew 5:21, 22. Now as you continue in the verses, hold the mirror a little closer.

Change some of the words to suit your life. For example,

- Proverbs 22:5 The path of the_____ (gossipers, tax cheaters, flirts, over-indulgers, mockers, or greedy guys) are snares and pitfalls, but those who would preserve their life stay far from them.
- Proverbs 29:25 The fear of_____ (tomorrow, teenager's arrival home, poverty, losing reputation, ill-health, or the bully) brings a snare, but whoever trusts in the Lord will be safe.
- Psalm 141:10 Let the _____ (boasters, grumps, poor listeners, me-first types, lazy ones, or angry drivers) fall into their own nets, while I escape safely.

Does this sound familiar: "You reap what you sow"? There are consequences to your choices. At every age, you and I need to be reminded of this. Underline the metaphorical description of what happens to your feet in the verses. God's purpose is guaranteed; He wants you to pay attention so that He can alter the way you are walking through life. If your sins have gotten you into trouble, talk them over with Him. Escape the trap. Get out of the pit. Throw off what hinders your walk with God.

FOLLOWING THROUGH: I take three steps.

In the deep, dark pit you pictured yourself in; you were looking up and calling for help. This is what prayer is, in a nutshell. Step one and step two, at least. Now that you and God have each other's attention, what do you do next?

A third step will help you remember that getting out of the traps gets your feet going in a new direction. This step is repentance. Clear the air and talk with God about what you've done. He knows already. He is just looking for your understanding of it and your agreement with what He saw happening. His goal is always is always to get you out of the trap; He wants you to walk in freedom. "Repent" means "to turn away from something" and "to turn back to God". It's all in the footwork!

When you are stuck, no matter how it happened:

Step One: Look up
Step Two: Call for help
Step Three: Repent

Now you can walk away from the trap, in a new direction and in the freedom He gave you.

31

Stumbling, Tripping and Falling

If you don't pay attention to your feet, you can suddenly stumble, trip, and even fall. Walking often entails consciously going around or over obstacles. In this devotion, you reflect on paying attention to your spiritual footwork.

Psalm 37:23, 24 (NLT)

The LORD directs the steps of the godly. He delights in every detail of their lives. Though they stumble, they will never fall, for the LORD holds them by the hand.

Psalm 73:1–3 (ESV)

Truly God is good to Israel, to those who are pure in heart. But as for me, my feet almost stumbled, my steps had nearly slipped. For I was envious of the arrogant and when I saw the prosperity of the wicked.

Psalm 119:165 (NLT)

Those who love your instructions have great peace and do not stumble.

Proverbs 4:11, 12 (NKJV)

I have taught you the way of wisdom; I have led you in right paths. When you walk, your steps will not be hindered, and when you run you will not stumble.

Proverbs 24:16a (NLT)

The godly may trip seven times, but they will get up again.

Proverbs 24:17, 18 (NLT)

Don't rejoice when your enemies fall; don't be happy when they stumble. For the LORD will be displeased with you and will turn His anger away from them.

Isaiah 3:8 (NLT)

For Jerusalem will stumble and Judah will fall, because they speak out against the LORD and refuse to obey him.

Romans 14:13 (NLT)

So let's stop condemning each other. Decide instead to live in such a way that you will not cause another believer to stumble and fall.

Hebrews 12:12, 13 (NLT)

So take a new grip with your tired hands and strengthen your week knees. Mark out a straight path for your feet so that those who are weak and lame will not fall but will become strong.

ENTERING: Losing your footing

I remember the last time I tripped and fell. I still have the bruise and scraped knee. A good conversation distracted me on a rocky desert trail; I wasn't looking straight ahead. I should have been more attentive to the path and to my feet. Can you remember your last stumble? What got in your way? How did you get back up on your feet?

Some wrong moves can have big spiritual consequences. The one time Adam and Eve turned away from God left a fallen legacy for all generations to come. Their weakness is mine and yours as well. The "Fall" is a baseline metaphor for sin. You can trace all faulty footwork to that first wrong move.

Look up "fall" in the dictionary and see how much vocabulary resounds with the fallout from that original sin. Samples from the Oxford Reference Dictionary:

- "Fall away" means to desert or vanish.
- "Fall back" means to retreat.
- "Fall flat" means to fail.
- A "fall guy" is an easy victim or scapegoat.

The unplanned physical moves of stumbling, tripping, and falling are a picture of the human spiritual condition after that first momentous "fall." Thankfully, God doesn't leave you in this predicament. He reverses the effects of the "fall" with His own resurrection. He gives you His Spirit so you can walk with your eyes on Him.

Quiet your inner spirit as you enter this devotion. Ask God for a revelation of His goodness, mercy, and sovereignty over your footwork. He is in control; His plan is a path forward and He is on it with you.

WALKING: Watching your step

Be careful as you move through these verses. There are people lying on the ground everywhere! Let the Word of God be your light. Pause and ask the Spirit of God to accompany you.

As you read through the first time, underline all the footwork terms. Then draw a circle around what causes the stumbling, tripping, and falling. Finally, highlight what prevents these faulty moves. Notice how your heart comes into play, one way or the other. What words describe the condition of your heart? Do they prompt you to say a quick prayer?

On your second reading, study God's specific role in this faulty footwork. Find the verse or verses where He provides:

- correction
- direction
- instruction
- protection
- rescue
- retribution
- support

Find one verse to help you remember to keep your eyes on God as you walk today.

FOLLOWING THROUGH: Leaning on God

For a moment, step into some uncomfortable shoes. This exercise will help you become more merciful and conscious of needing God's help with your own footwork.

Picture yourself with a broken foot after an accident. Even after surgery, full movement, balance, and weight-bearing seem like elusive goals. Apart from needing help every time you stumble, what else would you ask God for? How much would you lean on God for what you need?

Next, picture yourself as the victim of an explosion in a war zone where you live. You lost your foot. Amputation and crutches are now a reality. The ground you walk on is still dangerous. How much do you lean on God for what you need?

And finally, you are bedridden. You are very near the end of life. You remember what it was like to be on your feet, but now you walk only in your dreams. Jesus always joins you. He supports your inner spirit, making sure you don't stumble, trip, or fall. How much do you lean on Him for what you need?

As you reflect on these scenarios, remember this question: How much do you lean on God as you walk?

32

Turning away from God

When you take one step away from God, it is a significant move. Your heart dictates the decision. Your feet follow your heart, taking you in another direction.

Deuteronomy 5:32 (NIV 1984)

So be careful to do what the LORD your God has commanded you; do not turn aside to the right or to the left.

Isaiah 17:10b (NLT)

You have turned from the God who can save you.

Isaiah 53:3b (NLT)

We turned our backs on him and looked the other way. He was despised and we did not care.

Isaiah 59:13a (NLT)

We know we have rebelled and have denied the LORD. We have turned our backs on our God.

Jeremiah 2:19 (NLT)

Your wickedness will bring its own punishment. Your turning from me will shame you. You will see what an evil, bitter thing it is to abandon the LORD your God and not to fear him.

Jeremiah 2:27b (NLT)

"They turn their backs on me, but in times of trouble they cry out to me, 'Come and save us!'"

Jeremiah 3:19 (NLT)

"I thought to myself, 'I would love to treat you as my own children!' I wanted nothing more than to give you this beautiful land—the finest possession in the world. I looked forward to your calling me Father, and I wanted you never to turn from me."

Hebrews 10:38, 39 (NLT)

"And my righteous ones will live by faith. But I will take no pleasure in anyone who turns away." But we are not like those who turn away from God to their own destruction. We are the faithful ones, whose souls will be saved.

ENTERING: Saying no to God

Rejection can be an agonizing experience, especially on the receiving side. In the range of ways that rejection plays out, saying no at a dinner table may seem insignificant. It does, however, offer insight into what saying no to God means.

Picture yourself at a friend's house for dinner and your host offers you a second serving. In observing conventional manners, you would soften the no, offer thanks, and give a brief explanation. For example,

"No thank you, I have enjoyed everything but I have had plenty." Does this sound like your voice in that situation? What would your typical "no" response be? These days, common courtesy has shifted; "No thank you" has been replaced in some repertoires by "I'm good" or "I'm fine." I don't follow the logic in these expressions. Indeed, I wonder at the lack of politeness. You may have also noticed this shift.

When God invites people to be with Him, to walk with Him, or to eat with Him, some say "no" or just ignore the offer. Not just "No thank you, I believe in other gods," or "No thank you, I am busy with my life right now." But also "No, I'm good" or "I'm fine" or "I'm okay." Bad manners in the presence of the King of Kings aside, I think I see their logic. Some people think that they are okay, fine, and good without God! Their reasoning defies the eternal consequences of their response. What are your thoughts on this comparison?

Pause and reflect on when you recently said no to God. Maybe it was an opportunity to help someone, a discipline to train you, or perhaps a comfort to console you. Confess what was in your heart. What reason did you have for saying no?

WALKING: Going in a different direction

As you read through the scriptures notice how "turning away" is a clear body-language message. Say each verse aloud; then close your eyes and picture the turning action. Hold onto each verse long enough to imagine the accompanying actions and attitudes. Can you hear the "No thank you, I am good"? How does God respond to people turning away? Remember, Jesus experienced rejection; it was part of His suffering on earth. It was also His "red line": "*Whoever rejects the Son will not see life*" (John 3:36b NIV 1984).

Read the scriptures again slowly. Try to identify with the different voices. Each verse tells a very short story of turning away from truth and the consequences. Not all the results are bad; God is in the rescue business. In the margins alongside, note the different speakers, perhaps advisor, rebel, or God. Which voice sounds like you? Which voice sounds like someone speaking to you? Spend time contemplating what you have found, praying for God to step in.

Finally, create a very informal mind map to show the lessons in these verses connect. On a piece of paper, draw a circle in the center labeled "Turning away from God." Draw five circles around the central one, labeling them

- What this physically looks like
- What you get
- What you don't get
- Why you shouldn't
- What attitudes accompany this

Match the verses with the circles. Connect the circles in any way that the Spirit of God leads you to. Spend some time doodling while you further contemplate what the Holy Spirit is emphasizing. Highlight or double circle what compels you to pray. Jesus will come alongside you in that prayer.

FOLLOWING THROUGH: Following the trajectory

Your choices take you places. Turning away from God takes you in another direction, onto another path where you are not good, okay, or fine.

Think of someone you know who has turned his back on God, where he is now and where he is headed. You could draw this on paper too. His choices may line up in a logical way as a trajectory towards a certain direction. Does the biblical principle of reaping what you sow apply? How do you pray for him? Remember, God is the rescue business.

33

Walking in Darkness

The sheer number of verses in this devotion stresses how crucial this topic is to God. His truth cannot be concealed.

Genesis 1:4 (NIV)

God saw that the light was good, and he separated the light from the darkness.

Job 34:21, 22 (NIV 1984)

"His eyes are on the ways of men; he sees their every step. There is no dark place, no deep shadow, where evildoers can hide."

Psalm 82:5 (NKJV)

They do not know, nor do they understand; they walk about in darkness.

Isaiah 59:7–10 (NLT)

Their feet run to do evil, and they rush to commit murder. They think only about sinning. Misery and destruction always follow them. They don't know where to find peace or what it means to be just and good. They have mapped out crooked roads, and no one who follows them knows a moment's peace. So there is no justice among us, and we know nothing about right living. We look for light but find only darkness. We look for bright skies but walk in gloom. We grope like the blind along a wall, feeling our way like people without eyes. Even at brightest noontime, we stumble as though it were dark. Among the living, we are like the dead.

Jeremiah 13:15, 16 (NIV 1984)

Hear and pay attention, do not be arrogant, for the LORD has spoken. Give glory to the LORD your God before he brings the darkness, before your feet stumble on the darkening hills. You hope for light, but he will turn it to thick darkness and change it to deep gloom.

Zephaniah 1:14a, 17 (NKJV)

The great day of the LORD is near; It is near and hastens quickly.... "I will bring distress upon men, And they shall walk like blind men, Because they have sinned against the LORD; Their blood shall be poured out like dust, And their flesh like refuse."

Matthew 15:14 (NKJV)

Let them alone. They are blind leaders of the blind. And if the blind leads the blind, both will fall into a ditch.

John 1:5 (NIV 1984)

The light shines in the darkness, but the darkness has not understood it.

John 11:9, 10 (NLT)

Jesus replied, "There are twelve hours of daylight every day. During the day people can walk safely. They can see because they have the light of this world. But at night there is danger of stumbling because they have no light."

John 12:35 (NLT)

Jesus replied, "My light will shine for you just a little longer. Walk in the light while you can, so the darkness will not overtake you. Those who walk in the darkness cannot see where they are going."

1 John 2:11 (NLT)

But anyone who hates another brother or sister is still living and walking in darkness. Such a person does not know the way to go, having been blinded by darkness.

ENTERING: Spiritual darkness

You probably haven't experienced true darkness. Can you picture the black hole that physicists speak of? You may be more familiar with gradations of light than total darkness. Imagine yourself in an unlit cave or mine shaft, a windowless room without light, or at night during a full-grid electrical power outage. Blind people know darkness better than those who see well. In this devotion you will notice that the Bible refers to blindness often.

You may have heard Chris Tomlin's song "Here I am to Worship" with the lyrics "Light of the world, you stepped down into darkness, opened my eyes, let me see."

The darkness Tomlin refers to is spiritual darkness. It has more in common with a black hole than a power outage. Please hold these words in your heart and contemplate what God wants to show you today. This is a very bleak selection of scripture; there is barely a shaft of light. But, it may be the route on which the Holy Spirit best convicts you. Begin with the simple prayer: "Open the eyes of my heart, Lord Jesus."

WALKING: Spiritual discernment

Darkness isn't just some other person's experience, it is yours as well. Temptation waits at thresholds of darkened doorways, inviting you to enter. You cross over with your "yes" to sin. The steps decline with every self-deception.

Hold Jesus' hand as you walk through this devotion. He isn't just your minder; He is in control of the light switch. Plus, He can see in the dark. Walking in darkness would be overwhelming but for God's sovereignty over light and dark. While He created both, He lives in one.

Begin with the verse from Genesis. While God doesn't want you to walk in darkness, He does want you to see what happens there. He has wrapped plenty of neon "Caution" tape around those spiritual black holes so you won't slip in. Caution is your first discernment.

In John 11, Jesus talks about day and night, a familiar set of contrasts, giving you a picture of the duality of good and evil. As you read all of the verses, underline how darkness compares to other states or conditions like "gloom" or "deep shadow." Circle the places where blindness is a repeated theme. What do you think Jesus wants you to understand in this?

Now make three lists. Use this as an opportunity to do some self-examination. This will lead to further discernment.

- First, find the reasons given for walking in darkness (e.g., "no justice or right living"). Write the list in pen. Then, in pencil, add reasons why you have ever walked in darkness.
- Second, discover what happens in the dark. In pen, make a list from the verses (e.g., "misery and destruction"). In pencil, add a few more point-form notes from your personal experience.
- Finally, in permanent marker, list references to God's sovereignty, paying close attention to the finality of darkness for evil (e.g., "evildoers cannot hide").

Spend a little extra quiet time with God, reviewing what you have written, thinking about different dark situations in life that you have gone through and left behind. Take a moment to thank God for moving you out.

FOLLOWING THROUGH: Spiritual sovereignty

God has ultimate control over the spiritual darkness you experience. His Son stepped into darkness of this world and overcame its hold on you and on me by shedding His blood. The Light of the World removed and replaced darkness, proving God's sovereignty.

Ask God to shine light on any spiritual darkness in your life that you may not recognize. Once again, ask God to open the eyes of your heart. Speak the words you wrote in pencil as you pray, and repent of any separation you have had from God. Listen for His loving, life-giving, gloriously forgiving reply. With Jesus' hand in yours again, use an eraser to remove all the pencil marks.

34

Wandering

In this devotion, you will reflect on loved ones who have wandered from their spiritual home or their family home, or possibly both. As part of the exercise, you will have an opportunity to write a love letter to the wanderer you are missing.

Deuteronomy 30:1b–3 (NLT)

When you are living among the nations to which the LORD your God has exiled you, take to heart all these instructions. If at that time you and your children return to the LORD your God, and if you obey with all your heart and all your soul all the commands I have given you today, then the LORD your God will restore your fortunes. He will have mercy on you and gather you back from all the nations where he has scattered you.

2 Kings 21:8a (NKJV)

And I will not make the feet of Israel wander anymore from the land which I gave their fathers – only if they are careful to do according to all that I have commanded them.

Psalm 56:8 (NKJV)

You number my wanderings; Put my tears into Your bottle; Are they not in Your book?

Proverbs 21:16 (NKJV)

A man who wanders from the way of understanding will rest in the assembly of the dead.

Jeremiah 14:10 (NKJV)

They have loved to wander; They have not restrained their feet. Therefore, the LORD does not accept them; He will remember their iniquity now, And punish their sins.

Hosea 9:17 (NIV 1984)

My God will reject them because they have not obeyed him; they will be wanderers among the nations.

Matthew 18:12 (NIV 1984)

What do you think? If a man owns a hundred sheep, and one of them wanders away, will he not leave the ninety-nine on the hills and go to look for the one that wandered off?

James 5:19, 20 (NLT)

My dear brothers and sisters, if someone among you wanders away from the truth and is brought back, you can be sure that whoever brings the sinner back will save that person from death and bring about the forgiveness of many sins.

1 Peter 2:25 (NLT)

Once you were like sheep who wandered away. But now you have turned to your Shepherd, the Guardian of your souls.

ENTERING: Preparing to write

Sometimes, reaching out to a loved one who has wandered away is hard. Something drew her to a distance and has kept her there. Years may have come and gone. Maybe you are still hurting from things said or done. Where to begin the conversation? Do you even know where to send a letter? Would your frankness unhinge an already fragile relationship? Should you wait until you are on your death bed to be bold?

You've tasted the desperation. You have cried out to God and asked Him to write a letter in the stars, asked Him to speak to your loved one through dreams. You've printed the "WELCOME HOME" sign many times, adding in small print, "All is forgiven."

Close your eyes and think back over ways you have wronged others and yet been forgiven. What happened in you when you received forgiveness? How did you know that God was there? And now here you are – the one exercising forgiveness. You have prepared the banquet, so to speak. But that person needs to receive an invitation.

The Holy Spirit takes your surrender of lost loved ones seriously. Praise God that He is at work in that precious life, though you cannot see it. The Holy Spirit's "Christ compass" directs wandering feet and hearts back onto the narrow path to Jesus. It's a big enterprise, and the Spirit of God is in control.

This same loving, merciful God will show you how to write a love letter to the lost through this devotion. And then He will enable you.

WALKING: Writing the letter

Walk through the verses once, holding God's hand. A pen is in His other hand. Your Heavenly Father will model an invitation to forgiveness and reconciliation for you. He will show you how to write the same kind of letter. You can see in this devotion that He knows that feet and hearts are prone to wandering. But remember, He is merciful.

Stop to rest; catch your breath. Inhale the breath of God deeply so that the peace of Christ pervades you as you read this letter. He opens with

> *Dear Child. I have loved you with my whole heart no matter where you have gone. There hasn't been one moment I haven't thought of you. I have numbered all your wanderings and put your tears in a bottle. I have searched for you on the hills and in the valleys. I long for your return. I will pour mercy over you and restore you in every way. Turn to me. Return to me. Can you hear me calling?*

Walk through the devotion again. Notice that while God longs for the wanderer, He also demands justice. Pause at the James verse and meditate on it before God continues the letter:

> *Child, I forgive all of your sins, every wrong turn you have taken. But I am a just God; My Son covered your disobedience with His perfect shed blood. I want you back. I want to gather you in my arms. Just speak up, I will hear you. Just say, "Here I am, Lord." Then be assured, I will run to you.*

(With His signature) *Your Heavenly Father.*

Look back at the verses. Compare it to the letter, underlining parts of the letter that quote or reflect words from the verses. Remember that some wanderers stay away. The Holy Spirit whispers "persevere in prayer" and bids you to reread God's letter with complete faith.

FOLLOWING THROUGH: Personalizing the letter

Consider rewriting the letter above but addressing yours to your wandering loved one. Use your own words, as you feel comfortable. Ask Jesus for courage and graciousness as you put your hope and your forgiveness into words. Be sure to spend some time quietly listening to the Holy Spirit for direction. Receive God's assurance that He bore and buried all your sins, and that it is in the new life He gave you that you can extend this invitation of return to your beloved. Here you go:

Dear Son, Friend, Aunt, Colleague, Neighbor,

Former Teacher, Mother, Golf Buddy...

35

Wrong Moves

Have you ever felt the power of persuasion to the point where you couldn't resist? Giving up your will is not God's will.

Exodus 23:2a (NLT)

You must not follow the crowd in doing wrong.

Proverbs 2:12, 13 (NLT)

Wisdom will save you from evil people, from those whose words are twisted. These men turn from the right way to walk down dark paths.

Proverbs 19:2b (ESV)

Whoever makes haste with his feet misses his way.

Isaiah 59:7, 8 (NIV 1984)

Their feet rush into sin; they are swift to shed innocent blood. Their thoughts are evil thoughts; ruin and destruction mark their ways. The way of peace they do not know; there is no justice in their paths. They have turned them into crooked roads; no one who walks in them will know peace.

Isaiah 65:2 (NIV 1984)

All day long I have held out my hands to an obstinate people, who walk in ways not good, pursuing their own imaginations.

Jeremiah 2:36a (NLT)

First here, then there – you flit from one ally to another asking for help.

Jeremiah 7:24 (NLT)

But my people would not listen to me. They kept doing whatever they wanted, following the stubborn desires of their evil hearts. They went backward instead of forward.

Philippians 3:18 (ESV)

For many, of whom I have often told you and now tell you even with tears, walk as enemies of the cross of Christ.

Revelation 2:4 (MSG)

But you have walked away from your first love – why? What's going on with you, anyway? Do you have any idea how far you've fallen? A Lucifer fall!

ENTERING: Counterfeit leadership

The charismatic leader Adolf Hitler created an evil political movement. His military forces goose-stepped onto a path of destruction, as he compelled his followers to shed innocent blood. By all accounts, he personified evil. He was a "bad actor" who led others to commit atrocities. Their wrong deeds were the outcome of following the wrong man. His magnetism swept a whole people off its feet and into a whirlwind of wrong moves.

"Charisma" is an attribute that the enemy of God sometimes co-opts for sinful purposes. What God intended was that "charisms," or special graces, would strengthen the Body of Christ. The Holy Spirit gives wisdom, knowledge, healing, prophecy and discernment, and many other gifts to believers for the good of the whole Body. If Hitler's adherents had experienced true charism, and not a counterfeit, their path would have been different.

You, like everyone else, are prone to making wrong moves. You can be persuaded to climb mountains that are too high or to run with a crowd at odds with God. Peer pressure is real. Counterfeit leaders lie. Free will can be overruled by mob mentality. Feet can stampede. In the middle of things going badly how do you change course?

If you catch a wrong move mid-stride or avoid it in the first place, it doesn't have the same power. This devotion points to God's purpose and presence in allowing wrong moves. His gift of prayer helps you lean on Him to redirect your wrong moves.

WALKING: Counter-ACTS strategy

In life and in this devotion, we need to identify bad actors and bad actions. Some strong words describe God's opponents. As you read through the verses the first time, circle actors and underline actions. Pause after each verse and notice how feet get caught up or even cause the commotion. Open yourself to being persuaded by God to join Him in His ways and to be blessed by His charisms.

On second reading, go slowly. Select one or two verses that kindle a memory of a personal wrong move. This will help you pray specifically, using ACTS, a model of short prayers. ACTS is an acronym for

- Adoration. God's characteristics prompt your praise.
- Confession. The Holy Spirit convicts you of wrong moves.

- Thanksgiving. Expressions of gratitude to God bring you into His presence.
- Supplication. Presenting your needs to God, as He wants you to.

For example, my prayer through ACTS using Exodus 23:2a is as follows:

- I praise You, Heavenly Father, that Your Spirit helps me follow Jesus.
- I repent for the many times I have followed a group that I thought would build me up.
- Thank You that I am now learning to be content as someone different from "the crowd."
- Please, Father, help me make the right choices of people to spend time with.

Be alert as you pray for God's presence and purposes. Your submission to God will override any ill intention the enemy had in your wrong move.

Consider your lifestyle for a moment and ponder why "rushing" is included in a couple of verses. Also check out Daniel 12:4 (NLT).

FOLLOWING THROUGH: Contradict lies

Who said you were stuck in the last wrong move you made? Since when do your actions create permanent conditions? Doesn't God have the final say in your life? Don't His spiritual blessings have a real effect on how you live?

Remember, the enemy will use every choice or move you make to twist truth. God will never walk away from you. No matter what wrong moves you have made, returning to Him is always possible. He loves you and cares about your choices. It is up to you to say "no." Pivot away from sin. Make a step toward God. He wants a comeback in your life.

VIII

Devotion on Holy Ground – *Walking in God's Power*

36

At His Feet

In ancient days, people sat at the feet of their teachers. Those at Jesus' feet could testify to His divine interventions on their behalf.

During Jesus' earthly ministry

Mark 5:22–23a (NKJV)

And behold, one of the rulers of the synagogue came, Jairus by name. And when he saw Him, he fell at His feet and begged Him earnestly, saying, "My little daughter lies at the point of death. Come and lay Your hands on her, that she may be healed, and she will live."

Luke 10:39 (ESV)

And [Martha] had a sister called Mary, who sat at the Lord's feet and listened to his teaching.

John 11:32 (NKJV)

Then, when Mary came where Jesus was, and saw Him, she fell down at His feet, saying to Him, "Lord, if You had been here, my brother would not have died."

Matthew 15:30 (NKJV)

Then great multitudes came to Him, having with them the lame, blind, mute, maimed, and many others; and they laid them down at Jesus' feet, and He healed them.

Luke 17:16 (NLT)

[A healed leper] fell to the ground at Jesus' feet, thanking him for what he had done. This man was a Samaritan.

After Jesus' resurrection

Matthew 28:9 (NKJV)

And as they went to tell His disciples, behold, Jesus met them, saying, "Rejoice!" So they came and held Him by the feet and worshiped Him.

After Jesus' ascension

Revelation 1:13, 15, 17 (NKJV)

I saw ... One like the Son of Man, clothed with a garment down to the feet.... His feet were like fine brass, as if refined in a furnace.... And when I saw Him, I fell at His feet as dead. But He laid His right hand on me, saying to me, "Do not be afraid; I am the First and the Last." (This description of feet is repeated in Revelation 2:18)

Old Testament psalm

Psalm 99:5 (NLT)

Exalt the LORD our God! Bow low before His feet, for he is holy!

ENTERING: Find your feet in a new place

Imagine with a sigh of relief that you have come home. Quiet your thoughts as you prepare to enter this time of devotion with God. Take off your shoes if you like. Anticipate receiving a gift from God.

Along the way today you will see different scenes with one common focus – Jesus' feet. They are still. Some would say that His feet are a place, like a refuge.

Ask the Holy Spirit to bring to mind your pressing needs, heart's desires, or relevant memories as you go along. No need to suppress them. They will enrich the journey through the passage. Pray that God will give you what He wants you to receive.

WALKING: Slow down enough to see what is happening

Read the verses out loud slowly. Imagine Jesus' feet in the different settings. Imagine the activities under way in each scene. Get a sense of the patterns: what is asked for, what is given, what is received.

Returning to the verses, did you notice that difficult human conditions are welcome at Jesus' feet? Sometimes the conditions get reversed and healing happens. When you take time to linger there, inhibitions can be washed away by a wave of humility. Jesus' holiness changes you.

How do you think if felt to have his feet handled by friends, let alone strangers or enemies? His love eliminates barriers. You are supposed to bring your burdens to Him. If your heart is broken, His feet – with nail holes – are the perfect place to plead. You can be free to say anything, even if it is wrong. Wrongs can be reversed. Mary figured that out when her dead brother walked out of the grave.

Now read the verses out loud again. This time, imagine you are blindfolded and that the Holy Spirit has you by the hand. Concentrate on His voice whispering the words of scripture into your heart. (Did your heart skip a beat? Did your feet skip a little?) Find something that speaks to you and your life circumstances. Now, imagine yourself kneeling at the feet of Jesus. Reach out and touch them. What are you feeling as you kneel before Jesus? What is it you want to ask of Jesus? What is it you hope to receive?

Like Mary, you can chose to do the best thing by staying awhile at Jesus' feet. Surely, it is a compelling place of wonder, exaltation, and expectation. I hope you are leaving with something you needed.

FOLLOWING THROUGH: Remember you can return here

Feel free to linger awhile, and remember you can always return here. Some places on life's journey renew us. You simply need to return time and again. Jesus' feet are a place to stop and be still, a spiritual retreat. Your experience there begins and ends with the One who is First and Last.

These signs on the road direct you back to Jesus' feet:

- Worship here.
- Bring your desperation here.
- Exalt God here.
- Meet God face to face here.
- Experience His holiness here.
- Listen to His voice here.
- Come as you are.

When you find yourself in need but are struggling to settle in God's presence, imagine yourself sitting at the feet of Jesus. Hold on to His feet and pour out your heart to Him.

37

Barefoot on Holy Ground

In this devotion, you will reflect on encounters with God, through the story of Moses and the burning bush.

Exodus 3:1–12 (NIV)

Now Moses was tending the flock of Jethro his father-in-law, the priest of Midian, and he led the flock to the far side of the wilderness and came to Horeb, the mountain of God. There the angel of the LORD appeared to him in flames of fire from within a bush. Moses saw that though the bush was on fire it did not burn up. So Moses thought, "I will go over and see this strange sight—why the bush does not burn up."

When the LORD saw that he had gone over to look, God called to him from within the bush, "Moses! Moses!"

And Moses said, "Here I am."

"Do not come any closer," God said. "Take off your sandals, for the place where you are standing is holy ground." Then he said, "I am the God of your father, the God of Abraham, the God of Isaac and the God of Jacob." At this, Moses hid his face, because he was afraid to look at God.

The LORD said, "I have indeed seen the misery of my people in Egypt. I have heard them crying out because of their slave drivers, and I am concerned about their suffering. So I have come down to rescue them from the hand of the Egyptians and to bring them up out of that land into a good and spacious land, a land flowing with milk and honey—the home of the Canaanites, Hittites, Amorites, Perizzites, Hivites and Jebusites. And now the cry of the Israelites has reached me, and I have seen the way the Egyptians are oppressing them. So now, go. I am sending you to Pharaoh to bring my people the Israelites out of Egypt."

But Moses said to God, "Who am I that I should go to Pharaoh and bring the Israelites out of Egypt?"

And God said, "I will be with you. And this will be the sign to you that it is I who have sent you: When you have brought the people out of Egypt, you will worship God on this mountain."

ENTERING: Caught off guard

Your life may be full of social commitments. But in certain seasons of life, like Moses, you look for places to be alone. You hanker for solitary tasks and ways to blend purposefully into landscapes. You want your thoughts to be your own and for a time, your sense of self undisputed. Can you imagine God interrupting that kind of inconspicuous life?

Suddenness is one of God's signature timings. Being caught off guard means you can't prepare for what happens next. In fact, your automatic response is to focus on what is happening. How like God to find a way to take your eyes off yourself so that you have to zero in on Him. Moses got the burning bush. I wonder what experience God would design to rivet your attention on Him.

God's surprises always have a purpose. Think about His appearance and the most memorable parts of the conversation. He asked Moses to remove his footwear. Why would He want Moses to be barefoot? As you prepare to enter this devotion for a walk and talk with God, take off your shoes and socks. Go barefoot and link this physical state to the symbolism of baring your heart before God.

WALKING: Close to the fire

Read the passage once. As you do, step into Moses' sandals, taking on his thoughts and responses. Trace his footwork in this passage. Do his movements define him? What do they tell you about him? Does Moses' footwork reveal anything about his interlocutor, God? What future moves does God ask of Moses?

On your second reading, focus on the burning bush. Close your eyes and contemplate how God chose to show Himself. Make a list of words or expressions to describe the bush. For example,

- hot
- fascinating
- miraculous

Draw a simple picture of a burning bush beside the list. Do these words describe your image of God? Why would God choose to associate Himself with these characteristics? Like Moses, would you boldly approach and start asking questions? Why would God tell Moses not to come any closer?

On your third reading, think about where Moses was standing. God told him to take off his sandals because it was holy ground. Do you think it had always been a special area or did God's presence make the difference? Why would God ask Moses to remove his footwear? Your feet are very sensitive; pores and nerve-endings act as conduits to the rest of your body. What kind of sensory experience could Moses have had through his feet?

On your final reading, pay attention to what God said and how He spoke. In spite of the suddenness, Moses sounded ready. What would your first words be if God called your name aloud? God's big plans were a surprise. Moses went from staring at his bare feet to metaphorically putting on a very big pair of shoes. Would you feel up to the task? God's promise "I will be with you" should reassure you as you move forward with faith in God's strength alone.

Has God given you a glimmer of His burning bush presence in your life as you read and reread this passage?

FOLLOWING THROUGH: Continuous preparation

This passage is a snapshot of one event in Moses' life. Exodus 2 provides earlier insights into God's preparation of Moses' feet: being rescued, escaping, living on the run as a fugitive, being a rescuer of others, leading his flock of sheep in the wilderness. In spite of Moses' protestations (which continue in Exodus 3:13–4:17) God had always been preparing Moses to lead the Israelites in their escape and "life on the run" in the wilderness.

Patterns in our lives repeat themselves. Does Moses' story remind you of any patterns of movement in your life? Reflect on these and ask the Holy Spirit for deeper insight into how God has been preparing you. Ask also for an understanding of the ground you are on now and what God is calling you to.

I wonder if later in life Moses recalled that holy ground experience whenever he looked at his feet. His lowliest part left an imprint on holy ground. How like God to say profound things in simple ways! What stories would your feet tell? What has God been preparing them to do?

If they aren't off already, take off your shoes and close your eyes, ask God for a tactile sense of His presence.

38

Footstool of God

God lives in your heart. The concept of God's footstool invites you to visualize that He is at home there, resting His feet and bidding you to approach.

1 Chronicles 28:2 (ESV)

Then King David rose to his feet and said: "Hear me, my brothers and my people. I had it in my heart to build a house of rest [the Temple] for the ark of the covenant of the LORD and for the footstool of our God, and I made preparations for building."

2 Chronicles 9:18a (NIV 1984)

The throne [in the Temple] had six steps, and a footstool of gold was attached to it.

Psalm 99:5 (NIV 1984)

Exalt the LORD our God and worship at his footstool; he is holy.

Psalm 132:7 (NIV 1984)

Let us go to his dwelling place; let us worship at his footstool.

Isaiah 66:1 (NLT)

This is what the LORD says: "Heaven is my throne, and the earth is my footstool. Could you build me a temple as good as that? Could you build me such a resting place?"

Ezekiel 43:7a (NIV 1984)

He said: "Son of man, this is the place of my throne and the place for the soles of my feet. This is where I will live among the Israelites forever."

Hebrews 10:12, 13 (ESV)

But when Christ had offered for all time a single sacrifice for sins, he sat down at the right hand of God, waiting from that time until his enemies should be made a footstool for his feet.

ENTERING: Instilling a vision

Imagine God handing someone a blueprint to build a house for His presence on earth. King David received one for the Temple in Jerusalem. God wanted a dwelling place among His people. His instructions were very specific, right down to furnishing it with a footstool!

This simple piece of furniture might go unnoticed in most houses. But it is central to God's home – the place to meet and worship Him. Perhaps by its repeated presence and increasing significance in scripture, God wants you to envision the fulfillment of His Kingdom on earth. Could His footstool represent how His Kingdom plans would unfold? What is the future role for His footstool? This devotion traces the importance and the magnitude of this metaphor. God's footstool means the world to Him.

Approach God at His footstool and pray for insight with a prayer like this: "Lord, I want to learn how much this footstool means to you, so that I can understand how much it means to me."

WALKING: Installing a footstool

Ask the Holy Spirit to stretch your imagination as you contemplate what you cannot see but what He wants to reveal in this devotion. God's footstool does not fit in a box. It appears to be proportional to the size of His dwelling places.

Read through all the verses once. Trace the image of the footstool: its physical location and appearance, its spiritual functions, and then its supernatural dimensions. What is the Holy Spirit saying to your inner spirit about these descriptions? Are you awestruck?

On your second reading, contemplate the two verses from the Psalms, placing yourself at God's footstool. Imagine that His feet are resting there. Exalt God – He is so magnificent and yet so personal. Stay there until you sense His pleasure. Why do you think your closeness is so important to Him? Can you imagine His hand extended to you, drawing you even closer?

On your third time through the verses, consider the dimensions of God's footstool. Why would it be so big? What is the spiritual symbolism?

- What does "the earth is God's footstool" tell you about God's size?
- What does "a place for the soles of God's feet" say about His desire to live with His children?
- What does "the time until His enemies should be made a footstool for His feet" signify who will be triumphant in the end?

Spend some time meditating on the themes of dwelling, rest, and worship that arise in these verses. Contemplate the Hebrews verse as a culmination of these themes.

Pretend for a moment, that you are helping God build His next house. Ask Him whether the footstool is optional. What! Why would it be so indispensable?

FOLLOWING THROUGH: Indwelling His people

God's footstool must be in His house, as per His requirements. Now, ask yourself:

- Is Jesus enthroned in my heart (my inner spirit)? Does He have sole position on the footstool?
- Do I have any interior design issues I want to discuss with Him?

As you stand or kneel in worship at His footstool, trust God to continually show you the deep recesses of your being and His loving knowledge of how He has made you.

39

God's Feet

The Bible often depicts God as having physical qualities – including having feet. In this devotion, glimpses of His feet portray how supernatural He is.

Exodus 24:9, 10 (NLT)

Then Moses, Aaron, Nadab, Abihu, and the seventy elders of Israel climbed up the mountain. There they saw the God of Israel. Under his feet there seemed to be a surface of brilliant blue lapis lazuli, as clear as the sky itself.

Psalm 18:9 (NLT)

He opened the heavens and came down; dark storm clouds were beneath his feet.

Psalm 77:19, 20 (ESV)

Your way was through the sea, your path through the great waters; yet your footprints were unseen. You led your people like a flock by the hand of Moses and Aaron.

Nahum 1:3 (NKJV)

The LORD is slow to anger and great in power, And will not at all acquit the wicked. The LORD has His way in the whirlwind and in the storm, And the clouds are the dust of His feet.

Zechariah 14:4 (NIV 1984)

On that day his feet will stand on the Mount of Olives, east of Jerusalem, and the Mount of Olives will be split in two from east to west, forming a great valley, with half of the mountain moving north and half moving south.

Revelation 1:13, 15 (NIV 1984)

And among the lampstands was someone "like a son of man," dressed in a robe reaching down to his feet and with a golden sash around his chest.... His feet were like bronze glowing in a furnace, and his voice was like the sound of rushing waters.

ENTERING: A glimpse of His feet

God's feet should intrigue you. They are His most-oft appearing body part in His Word. Now, feet – in the natural scheme – are the lowest member of the body, the subject of taboos and superstition. God knows that. God uses the humble to reveal what is holy.

When He shows you His feet, He shows you His glory; the Jewish idiom *Ragle Shekinah* means "the feet of His presence." Metaphors in the Bible are pictures of truth that God wants us to grasp.

Close your eyes and ask God to show you that the place of His feet is glorious (Isaiah 60:13b NKJV).

WALKING: A glimpse of His glory

Pretend that you have ample financial resources and want to commission a portrait of God's feet. Walk with the Holy Spirit so He can help you choose one of the verses from which to model the picture. What fun!

You want the artist to draw or paint God's feet, no other parts of Him. As you walk through the first time, pause at each verse to get a glimpse of God's presence. Pay particular attention to His feet in the different scenes.

Get ready to take consultation notes on:

- setting
- actions
- parts that are difficult to imagine or depict

Read the verses again, noting details from each verse. For example, in Psalm 18 you find the following:

- setting – heavens open, dark storm clouds
- actions – descending from above but feet remaining on the clouds
- parts that are difficult to imagine or depict – is the opening in heaven a door?

On your third reading, go very slowly. You are getting ready to make a choice. Visualize each verse. What does each one tell you about His feet? What would a depiction of natural, physical feet tell you about the supernatural, spiritual God?

Finally, ask the Holy Spirit to put you in each picture. Which one draws you closer to God's feet? Then step outside that picture and imagine looking at the picture with Jesus. What is He saying to you?

FOLLOWING THROUGH: A gallery of God's presence

Consider these additional exercises to help you retain the imagery of these verses:

1. Print each verse or just your favorite verse about God's feet on a single sheet of paper in large font. Pin up the sheet and familiarize yourself with it. Each time you walk by the sheet, imagine the scene, God's feet, and all the activity – natural and supernatural. Ponder what is difficult to depict.

2. Commission a child you know who can draw unselfconsciously. Read your chosen verse to him or her and talk simply about the details you would like to see in the picture. Post the picture on your fridge, to meditate upon as you work in the kitchen.

40

Taking Territory

Walking with God accomplishes His purposes to transform your life. Through you, He also transforms your community and the very land you walk on.

Genesis 13:17 (MSG)

"So – on your feet, get moving! Walk through the country, its length and breadth; I'm giving it all to you."

Deuteronomy 2:5 (NIV 1984)

Do not provoke them to war, for I will not give you any of their land, not even enough to put your foot on.

Deuteronomy 11:22–24a (NLT)

Be careful to obey all these commands I am giving you. Show love to the LORD your God by walking in his ways and holding tightly to him. Then the LORD will drive out all the nations ahead of you, though they are much greater and stronger than you, and you will take over their land. Wherever you set foot, that land will be yours.

Joshua 1:3 (NLT)

"I promise you what I promised Moses: 'Wherever you set foot, you will be on land I have given you.'"

Joshua 14:9b (NIV)

"'The land on which your feet have walked will be your inheritance and that of your children forever, because you have followed the LORD my God wholeheartedly.'"

ENTERING: Feet bring presence

All over the world, prayer walkers reclaim their streets as territory for Jesus. They pray as they pass by their neighbors' homes, their schools, and local businesses. They walk the perimeters where crime or violence occur and anoint the corners with holy water or oil. The Holy Spirit calls them to the task and leads them.

Sometimes, they simply ask God to bless the occupants. If they know of a real need, they intercede, asking God to meet that need. If they know of trouble, they ask Jesus to meet it head on. Intercessors have witnessed individuals and communities come to faith in Christ. They submit their prayers and conscious footwork to God. By bringing the presence of God with them, they are changing the spiritual atmosphere. Jesus did the same thing when He walked the earth.

God calls some intercessors to pray for people in faraway places. They may not always understand the reasons or be able to pray specifically. He fills their hearts with a passion for a people and a place they may have never encountered. Ruth Ward Heflin, a missionary to Jerusalem, learned that moving her feet during prayer and praise brought an outpouring of the Holy Spirit. She danced on maps of faraway places. Later, God led her to those places to see what He was doing.[2]

---

[2]   Ruth Ward Heflin, *Glory* (McDougall, 1990).

The prayer walkers could have stayed at home and prayed. The intercessors might have just touched the map on a wall while praying. But they didn't. What difference did their feet bring? What happens when you use your feet purposefully in prayer? As we enter this devotion, ask God to help you understand the spiritual impact your feet make on earth.

WALKING: Feet take territory

Read the verses and listen to God speaking to the Jewish nation about the land they will possess in His name. If you are a Gentile (non-Jewish) believer, read the scripture again with the understanding that "taking territory" is also a metaphor for the spiritual territory that God wants you to stand on and possess (Ephesians 6:13).

Open yourself to the possibility of prayer walking in your local community. Read the verses through again. Notice how God warns, instructs, and gives permission. Highlight the ones that challenge you. Look for God's plans to accomplish peace and for the importance of staying close to Him. Pay attention to His prompts inside of you. Do ideas come to mind of where He wants you to set your feet?

Circle the verses that give permission to take territory. Notice that God makes a simple declaration and it is done. Submit your heart, your feet, and your target area to the Lord for His purposes. Rephrase the verses, personalizing each one with your name and location, asking God for permission. Are your feet poised to move?

FOLLOWING THROUGH: Feet accompany faith

Consider taking a purposeful walk with a praying friend around your neighborhood. Pray a blessing on your feet and heart and then ask the Holy Spirit to take you where He wants you to go. Ask Him what He wants you to notice. Keep up an internal running prayer of thanksgiving. Pay attention to any encounters and the gist of any unexpected conversations. Use encouraging words to bless others. Let the Holy Spirit "do the work" of taking territory for Christ.

41

Under God's Feet

Some footwork metaphors in the Bible portray God as warrior and victor. He is, after all, the Lord of Heaven's Armies. This devotion helps you understand what He is fighting for.

Psalm 60:12 (NIV 1984)

With God we will gain the victory, and he will trample down our enemies.

Micah 7:18, 19 (NLT)

Where is another God like you, who pardons the guilt of the remnant, overlooking the sins of his special people? You will not stay angry with your people forever, because you delight in showing unfailing love. Once again you will have compassion on us. You will trample our sins under your feet and throw them into the depths of the ocean!

1 Corinthians 15:24–26 (NIV 1984)

Then the end will come, when he hands over the kingdom to God the Father after he has destroyed all dominion, authority and power. For he must reign until he has put all his enemies under his feet. The last enemy to be destroyed is death.

Ephesians 1:22, 23 (NIV 1984)

And God placed all things under his feet and appointed him to be head over everything for the church, which is his body, the fullness of him who fills everything in every way.

Hebrews 2:7, 8 (NIV 1984)

"You made him a little lower than the angels; you crowned him with glory and honor and put everything under his feet." In putting everything under him, God left nothing that is not subject to him. Yet at present we do not see everything subject to him.

ENTERING: Press "Rewind" then "Stop"

In the Old Testament, enemy nations enslaved and oppressed Israel. God's people cried out for protection. He promised them a Messiah. Israel expected a warrior king to overcome their enemies. God intervened with military strength at different times: Gideon's tiny army won; David took down the giant Goliath; and Jehoshaphat's opponents killed each other. In these battles, God spiritually superintended Israel's victories. Israel's understanding was often limited to what they could see in the physical world.

In Ephesians 6:10–18, Paul says to put on the armor of God against the spiritual forces in the heavenly realm. His physical imagery describes God's provision in spiritual battles. Each part of the amour is a metaphor of a spiritual gift, an attribute; this is the language our unseen enemy understands.

Think about it: you have the same challenge as Israel. Living in the moment, putting little store in the eternal. But God gets your attention when problems overwhelm you. How do foreclosures, pedophiles, gun violence, and fraud get resolved on a spiritual level? You look for expedient solutions in the political and social spheres. Sometimes you see the hand of God. What you need to see are His feet! God's feet signal the enemy's defeat.

This devotion takes you on a video tour of God's footwork against His enemies. First, contemplate Zechariah 4:6 (NLT) "It is not by force nor by strength, but by my Spirit, says the Lord of Heaven's Armies." Now ask the Holy Spirit to accompany your personal study of "Under God's Feet". He is actually very gentle. Don't worry!

WALKING: Press "Play"

On your first reading, decide which verses are moving images of feet and which are still shots. Write: "moving" or "still" in the margins. Notice the verb tenses: some are past and some future. For example, I see

- Psalm 60:12 as a moving image
- Ephesians 1:22, 23 as a still image.

Let your second reading become a study session with your personal tutor. Just as the disciples asked Jesus to explain His parables (Matthew 13:36; 15:15), you can ask the Holy Spirit to explain what the metaphors mean in each verse. Look for explication in the rest of the verse. If it is still not clear, ask Him to tell you more. Go through each footwork metaphor:

- Trampling down our enemies means…
- Trampling our sins means…
- Putting his enemies under his feet means…
- Placing all things under his feet means…
- Putting everything under his feet means…

As your study session continues, put yourself in each frame. Consult the Holy Spirit about how these verses

- portray God's willingness to fight for you
- describe what the Lord of Heaven's Armies fights for and against on your behalf

Finally, ask the Holy Spirit to help you contemplate the footwork metaphor "under God's feet" in light of this verse: "But the Lord of Heaven's Armies will be exalted by his justice. The holiness of God will be displayed by his righteousness" (Isaiah 5:16, NLT).

FOLLOWING THROUGH: Press "Fast Forward"

Your greatest reward will be to see the feet of God resting upon a heavenly footstool. All of heaven and earth will be under His feet. The Bible gives us two glimpses of this setting. Both Isaiah and John (the beloved disciple) were taken up to heaven so that they could bring back a prophetic picture of what will be one day.

Before you leave this devotion altogether, and whenever you return, spend time worshipping God and celebrating His coming reign. Join with the angels and the saints as you call out together before the throne of God.

"Holy, holy, holy is the LORD of Heaven's Armies! The whole earth is filled with his glory!" (Isaiah 6:3b, NLT)

Everything is under His feet!

42

Under Your Feet

In this devotion, we look at the notion of trampling enemies underfoot as an invitation to focused prayer.

2 Samuel 22:37–39 (NKJV)

You enlarged my path under me; So my feet did not slip. I have pursued my enemies and destroyed them; Neither did I turn back again till they were destroyed. And I have destroyed and wounded them; So they could not rise; they have fallen under my feet.

1 Kings 5:3 (NKJV)

You know my father David could not build a house for the name of the LORD his God because of the wars which were fought against him on every side, until the LORD put his foes under the soles of his feet.

Psalm 44:5 (NKJV)

Through You we will push down our enemies; Through Your name we will trample down those who rise up against us.

Romans 16:20a (NIV 1984)

The God of peace will soon crush Satan under your feet.

ENTERING: Understood

There is powerful symbolism in flattening foes underfoot. Ancient Roman and Egyptian soldiers used to draw faces of their enemies on the soles of their sandals so they could literally step on them.[3] More recently, in the 1980s, General Manual Noriega, Panama's military-leader-turned-drug-lord, put the names of his rivals on paper and then inside his shoes. He walked on his enemies.[4] Now that Noriega is a professing Christian,[5] it would interesting to see if he has retained the habit.

The enemy of God copies this symbolic footwork in spiritual warfare. In 1600, authorities forced Japanese Christians to walk on pictures of Jesus or the Virgin Mary, severely testing their faith. Japanese historians refer to this period of trial as E-fumi (fumu means "to crush or step on"; e means "picture").[6]

The Bible offers examples of how God uses human feet to tread, trample, and crush His enemy. If this is a mutually understood body language on the battlefield of your spiritual life, this devotion provides a model for simple, on-target prayer. You supply the shoes.

WALKING: On faith

As you walk through this devotion with the Holy Spirit, know that God has a plan to use your feet in ways that you cannot see. Ask Him to build your faith that He will overcome the wiles of His enemy in your midst.

---

[3]   Linda O'Keefe, Shoes (Workman Publishing, 1997), p. 35.

[4]   Jon Ronson, The Men Who Stare at Goats (Simon & Schuster, 2004), quoted in "Good Reads" http://www.goodreads.com/review/show/23609547.

[5]   CNN July 8, 2007.

[6]   Wikipedia.

First, read through and be encouraged by all that God is doing. Underline all the things that God is doing for you:

- acting for you
- bringing peace
- controlling the timing
- crushing Satan
- enlarging your path
- fighting with you
- protecting your feet
- proving His sovereignty
- putting your enemies under your feet

As you go through the verses a second time. Select one or two that reflect your life. Do any of them trigger a target for prayer? For example, this might be your prayer:

"Lord, let me be entirely dependent on your work in and through me when I feel surrounded by enemy activity. Put it under my feet; defeat it, in Your Name I pray".

Finally, name what you need God to crush. Write it out on paper or write it on the bottom of your shoes. I wrote "sorrow" under my shoes. What will you write?

FOLLOWING THROUGH: Underfoot

An even greater offense in spiritual warfare is the use of the Word of God. An Arizona company called Walk by Faith sells flip flops with Bible verses imprinted on the soles, under your feet. "The die-cut bottom will imprint a message in dirt, sand or even a damp sidewalk. They allow you to testify without saying a word. When you walk you leave the Word of God behind for others to see."[7]

Remember, when your feet and faith are in motion, God is advancing His Kingdom. God is delivering messages under your feet that His enemy understands.

---

[7]   www.walkbyfaithaz.com

IX

Destination – *Following Jesus beyond the Narrow Gate*

43

Entering God's Kingdom

The footwork of entering is a single step, preceded and followed by other steps. But the foot that crosses a threshold declares "entry accomplished." And so it is when you enter the Kingdom of God.

Matthew 7:13–14 (NLT)

You can enter God's Kingdom only through the narrow gate. The highway to hell is broad, and its gate is wide for the many who choose that way. But the gateway to life is very narrow and the road is difficult, and only a few ever find it.

Matthew 7:21 (NIV 1984)

"Not everyone who says to me, 'Lord, Lord,' will enter the kingdom of heaven, but only he who does the will of my Father who is in heaven.

Matthew 19:24 (NIV 1984)

"Again I tell you, it is easier for a camel to go through the eye of a needle than for a rich man to enter the kingdom of God."

Matthew 23:13 (NIV 1984)

"Woe to you, teachers of the law and Pharisees, you hypocrites! You shut the kingdom of heaven in men's faces. You yourselves do not enter, nor will you let those enter who are trying to."

Mark 10:15 (NIV 1984)

"I tell you the truth, anyone who will not receive the kingdom of God like a little child will never enter it."

John 3:5 (NLT)

Jesus replied, "I assure you, no one can enter the Kingdom of God without being born of water and the Spirit."

John 10:9a (NIV 1984)

"I am the gate; whoever enters through me will be saved."

ENTERING: The gate

Gates were significant in ancient walled cities. Not only were they the only entrances and exits, gates were also meeting places for commercial, social, and legal activities. Civil authorities scrutinized the intentions of those entering, not unlike our current-day passport control. Citizens fortified their gates against invaders. Teachers and prophets gathered their followers to make pronouncements there. Gates were places where power and authority were on display. They continue to bear witness to footwork of all who pass through or gather there. The "gate" metaphor draws deep meaning from ancient times.

The commemoration of Passover each year recalls Israelites in Egypt marking their doorways with the blood of a slain lamb. The mark identified them as God's people so that the angel of death would spare them (Exodus 12:22, 23). Jews to this day put a sign on the gates of their cities and on their home's doorposts. The sign, called a *mezuzah*, is an excerpt of scripture from the Book of Deuteronomy. The occupants touch these signs when they enter and exit; they pause in their footwork intentionally. This act of touching a dedicated doorway symbolizes a heart consecrated to God. Indeed, the three Hebrew letters that spell the word "gate"—*ShUR*—have the distilled meaning: "The bringing forth for new birth a broken heart and contrite spirit for God's harvest." God ensured that gates were spiritually significant, an opening and a going-through, in the lives of the Jewish people. It was as if He set up a pattern of feet and hearts in-sync.

Jesus said "I am the gate." His contemporaries would have understood the gate metaphor readily. What about you – do have a ready understanding or are you ready for a revelation?

WALKING: The step

As you begin this devotion, slow yourself down so that you can acknowledge what a single step in your walk feels like. Ask the Holy Spirit to help you read and reread the passages. On your first reading, look for the synonyms for God's Kingdom. I found four. Underline them, and circle the word "enter" or its equivalent.

Given that people are allowed to pass through gates only by meeting certain criteria, read through the verses again, as though you were in charge of passport control. The first and last verses describe who may enter, and the middle five verses declare who may not. Make two lists on a separate piece of paper: "Qualified" and "Disqualified." Do two more exercises with these lists:

- Rewrite the "disqualified," negatively phrased verse as a positive, such as the following:
  ◦ Those who say 'Lord, Lord' and do the will of my Father in heaven will enter the kingdom of heaven.
  ◦ Those who receive the kingdom of God like a little child will enter it.

- Rewrite the "qualified," positively phrased verse as a negative, such as the following:
  - Those who do not enter through Jesus, the gate, will not be saved.

In this analogy of passport control, who do you think gives permission and stamps the identity card of the entrant?

Time to slow down; pick two verses to contemplate for five minutes with your eyes closed and your heart focused on Jesus. Afterward, recall your inner discussion and write a couple of sentences, starting with "I…"

Before leaving this devotion, look at your feet through spiritual eyes. Are you standing in the Kingdom of God? Think about when your entry took place. Reflect on the personal steps you took as you approached the gate. What one step took you through to God's Kingdom?

FOLLOWING THROUGH: The next step

Imagine that you have been given the assignment to run a "citizenship class" for future entrants into the Kingdom of God, based on this devotion.

- First, read Matthew 10 for an overview of how Jesus instructed His disciples on qualifying candidates.
- Then, in the same chapter, look for why it is so important to acknowledge Jesus when speaking to others.

44

Entering the Most Holy Place

This footwork metaphor deepens understanding of how it is possible for you to follow an ascended Savior from an earthly walk to a heavenly home. "On earth, as it is in heaven" is a prayer answered.

On earth

Hebrews 8:5a (NLT)

They serve in a system of worship that is only a copy, a shadow of the real one in heaven.

Hebrews 9:1–3, 6b–7 (NLT)

That first covenant between God and Israel had regulations for worship and a place of worship here on earth. There were two rooms in that Tabernacle.... [The first] room was called the Holy Place. Then there was a curtain, and behind the curtain was the second room called the Most Holy Place....

The priests regularly entered the first room as they performed their religious duties. But only the high priest ever entered the Most Holy Place, and only once a year. And he always offered blood for his own sins and for the sins the people had committed in ignorance.

Hebrews 9:8 (NIV 1984)

The Holy Spirit was showing by this that the way into the Most Holy Place had not yet been disclosed as long as the first tabernacle was still standing.

Matthew 27:50, 51a (NLT)

Then Jesus shouted out again, and he released his spirit. At that moment the curtain in the sanctuary of the Temple was torn in two, from top to bottom.

As it is in heaven

Hebrews 6:19, 20a (NLT)

This hope is a strong and trustworthy anchor for our souls. It leads us through the curtain into God's inner sanctuary. Jesus has already gone in there for us.

Hebrews 9:12 (NLT)

With his own blood—not the blood of goats and calves—he entered the Most Holy Place once for all time and secured our redemption forever.

Hebrews 9:24 (NLT)

For Christ did not enter into a holy place made with human hands, which was only a copy of the true one in heaven. He entered into heaven itself to appear now before God on our behalf.

Hebrews 10:19 (NLT)

And so, dear brothers and sisters we can boldly enter heaven's Most Holy Place because of the blood of Jesus.

ENTERING: Behind the curtain

Sin is real; the separation it causes between a holy God and His errant people is equally real. It seems, however that God chose symbolism to teach about and even to remove sin. Early on, God set up an earthly system of representation (with priests) and symbolic atonement (with sacrifices) that would foreshadow His future system.

In the Tabernacle and later the Temple, a curtain covered the entrance to the inner sanctum of the Most Holy Place. Significantly, God's presence was behind the curtain. The high priest alone could enter the Most Holy Place on behalf of the people and their sins. Once a year, he asked anew for mercy and reconciliation. It was a risky business to enter the Most Holy Place. The high priest had a rope tied to his ankle in case he died in God's presence. If that happened, his peers could pull him out (see Exodus 28:35 study note in NLT Study Bible).

God's system evolved as He had always planned: Jesus (the perfect substitute) and His death (the perfect sacrifice) would bridge the gulf between God and all humanity. This devotion connects the dots of how Jesus won the way for you to enter the Most Holy Place. No need for a rope around your ankle.

WALKING: Through the curtain

You are in! And now, you get to retrace the footsteps of Jesus, who made your entry possible. As you read through the verses slowly, pick up two pens. Using a black pen, underline these key words in the verses: "curtain," "enter," and "The Most Holy Place." Above the word "enter" write the word "feet." Using a red pen, underline "blood." Do you see a story forming of what God was doing in presenting truth symbolically?

On your second reading, pause to meditate on certain verses. What is the connection between Hebrews 9:8 and Matthew 27:50–51a? Contemplate God's masterful foreshadowing in: Hebrews 8:5a and Hebrews 9:24.

How did Jesus make a way for you to enter the Most Holy Place? Using your red pen, draw little footprints in the margin beside the last six verses (or draw hearts if you find drawing toes challenging). What do these red footprints symbolize?

Reread the verses one more time so that you feel like you know what God wants to tell: the story of redemption from sin and separation. In your own words, retell this story about entering the Most Holy Place. Use your underlining to recall how one system shifted to another better one. A free admission! Do you sense how huge a price Jesus paid for your entry?

FOLLOWING THROUGH: In His presence

Return to the last six verses with this responsorial psalm in your heart and a lift to your step. *"Enter his gates with thanksgiving and his courts with praise; give thanks to him and praise his name."* (Psalm 100:4 NIV 1984)

45

Standing in God's Presence

Qualifying to stand in God's presence requires meeting the highest standard of holiness. This devotion asks: "Who may stand?" and "On what basis?"

Deuteronomy 10:8 (NIV 1984)

At that time the LORD set apart the tribe of Levi to carry the ark of the covenant of the LORD, to stand before the LORD to minister and to pronounce blessings in his name, as they still do today.

Joshua 7:10 (NIV 1984)

The LORD said to Joshua, "Stand up! What are you doing down on your face?

1 Samuel 6:20b (NIV 1984)

"Who can stand in the presence of the LORD, this holy God?"

Psalm 101:7B (NIV 1984)

No one who speaks falsely will stand in my presence.

Ezekiel 22:30 (NIV 1984)

"I looked for a man among them who would build up the wall and stand before me in the gap on behalf of the land so I would not have to destroy it, but I found none."

Malachi 3:1, 2 (NIV 1984)

"See, I will send my messenger, who will prepare the way before me. Then suddenly the Lord you are seeking will come to his temple; the messenger of the covenant, whom you desire, will come," says the LORD Almighty. But who can endure the day of his coming? Who can stand when he appears? For, he will be like a refiner's fire or a launderer's soap.

Romans 14:10b–12 (NIV 1984)

For we will all stand before God's judgment seat. It is written: "'As surely as I live,' says the Lord, 'every knee will bow before me; every tongue will confess to God.'" So then, each of us will give an account of himself to God.

Jude 1:24, 25 (MSG)

And now to him who can keep you on your feet, standing tall in his bright presence, fresh and celebrating—to our one God, our only Savior, through Jesus Christ, our Master, be glory, majesty, strength, and rule before all time, and now, and to the end of all time.

Revelation 7:9 (NIV 1984)

After this I looked and there before me was a great multitude that no one could count, from every nation, tribe, people and language, standing before the throne and in front of the Lamb. They were wearing white robes and were holding palm branches in their hands.

ENTERING: Framing the question

Foreign-language teachers train their students to use essential communication tools. Framing a question is one of those tools. The 5Ws and H questions are

- Who
- What
- Where
- When
- Why
- How

The 5Ws and H questions are useful because they gather the most information. Journalists use these questions to guide their writing. This ensures that their readers get the full story.

Of the questions, "Who" prompts the most personal answer. The question, "Who can stand in the presence of God?" is important to God, to His people in the Bible, and to you. Bow your head and ask God who can stand in His presence.

WALKING: Framing the answer

Ask the Holy Spirit to help you engage in this devotion at a deep personal level. Read through the verses once. The question, "Who can stand in the presence of a holy God?" is asked in two ways. Find those verses and underline the questions. Think about the different wording. What do the additional details tell you? Will that information determine the answer?

Read through again. Notice that this question is an active search on God's part. Deepen your own enquiry about the people and experiences in God's presence. Add more questions. For example,

- What did the priests do as they stood before the Lord?
- How does the 1 Samuel verse help explain Joshua's reaction to God's presence?

- Who was God hoping would stand before Him in the gap? Why?
- What will happen when we all stand before God's judgment seat?
- Where do you hope you will ultimately stand before God?

Read the verses in their entirety once again. With a pen and paper or just in your mind, chart the progression of a timeline, past to future. Do you see a turning point from Ezekiel to Malachi? Does this answer the questions posed at the outset: "Who may stand?" and "On what basis?"

FOLLOWING THROUGH: Put yourself in the frame

What do the New Testament verses declare about God having answered His own question? Choose one of them to contemplate. Ask God if you may stand in His presence one day.

46

Standing in the Promised Land

An immigrant might kiss the ground of a new homeland. The Israelites marked their gratitude by standing on the boundary in the presence of God. Later, they honored the memory with stones from that unusual place.

Joshua 3:1–4a, 8, 13, 15–16a, 17 (NIV 1984)

Early in the morning Joshua and all the Israelites set out from Shittim and went to the Jordan, where they camped before crossing over. After three days the officers went throughout the camp, giving orders to the people: "When you see the ark of the covenant of the LORD your God, and the priests, who are Levites, carrying it, you are to move out from your positions and follow it. Then you will know which way to go, since you have never been this way before."…

[The Lord said to Joshua] "Tell the priests who carry the ark of the covenant: 'When you reach the edge of the Jordan's waters, go and stand in the river.'"…

And as soon as the priests who carry the ark of the LORD—the Lord of all the earth—set foot in the Jordan, its waters flowing downstream will be cut off and stand up in a heap."…

Now the Jordan is at flood stage all during harvest. Yet <u>as soon as</u> the priests who carried the ark reached the Jordan and <u>their feet touched the water's edge,</u> the water from upstream stopped flowing…. <u>The priests who carried the ark of the covenant of the LORD stood firm on dry ground in the middle of the Jordan, while all Israel passed by until the whole nation had completed the crossing on dry ground….</u>

Joshua 4:1–3, 6b–7, 15–18, 20–22 (NIV 1984)

When the whole nation had finished crossing the Jordan, the LORD said to Joshua, "Choose twelve men from among the people, one from each tribe, and tell them to take up <u>twelve stones from the middle of the Jordan from right where the priests stood</u> and to carry them over with you and put them down at the place where you stay tonight."…

"In the future, when your children ask you, 'What do these stones mean?' Tell them that the flow of the Jordan was cut off before the ark of the covenant of the LORD. When it crossed the Jordan, the waters of the Jordan were cut off. These stones are to be a memorial to the people of Israel forever."…

Then the LORD said to Joshua, "Command the priests carrying the ark of the Testimony to come up out of the Jordan." So Joshua commanded the priests, "Come up out of the Jordan." And the priests came up out of the river carrying the ark of the covenant of the LORD. <u>No sooner had they set their feet on the dry ground</u> than the waters of the Jordan returned to their place and ran at flood stage as before….

And Joshua set up at Gilgal the twelve stones they had taken out of the Jordan. He said to the Israelites, "In the future when your descendants ask their fathers, <u>'What do these stones mean?' tell them, 'Israel crossed the Jordan on dry ground.'"</u>

(Emphasis, mine)

ENTERING: Standing on His promise

One of God's many covenantal promises was to provide a homeland to Abraham's descendants. It wasn't a straightforward inheritance. His promise was eternal, but He delayed its fulfillment. As God revealed Himself to successive generations through Isaac and Jacob, He looked for faith and obedience in the hearts of His chosen people. It took a long and circuitous journey to get to the Promised Land. The nation of Israel endured the parallel physical and spiritual enslavement and much wandering. But a promise is a promise. In this passage, a more obedient generation finally arrives in the Promised Land. God stands on His promises; He keeps them. You can count on that.

Preparation is a strong theme in the Old Testament. The priests in these readings were direct descendants of Aaron, Moses' brother. They set themselves apart from the general population to serve God. It is of note that each received a special anointing of the blood of a sacrificed ram on the big toe of his right foot (Exodus 29:20). This consecration symbolically prepared them to walk differently in their service to God. Their feet would play a significant role in the final stage of the journey to Canaan, the Promised Land.

After a cursory reading of this passage, you might think that feet can cause miracles to happen. Quite the opposite. It was all God, all the time, managing the marvelous feats of dry river crossing "number two." After centuries of holding His promise in abeyance, God led His people to their Promised Land. Can you imagine the excitement that accumulated in the last days of being in the desert? Joshua must have had a few crowd-control issues.

WALKING: Memorializing His promise

Imagine that you are one of the people crossing the river Jordan. Ask the Holy Spirit to accompany you each step of the way. As you read through the first time, get a sense of the unfolding story and of the timeline. How many days do you think it would take you before, during, and after the crossing? Deliberate on this for a while, but prepare for more challenging questions.

On your second reading, imagine again that you are walking with your family. Describe your route. What is it like looking at the water of the Jordan as you cross on dry ground? What is the sensation, underfoot? Does the threat of the dam bursting take your eyes off the opposite shore? Do the priests seem to be straining as you pass them, or are they calm? Do you notice the rocks in the center of the river bed, or are they everywhere? Why do you think God asked the priests to stop and stay at the halfway point? What about you? How does this experience change or confirm your understanding, of who God is, and his plans for you and your people? What feelings did you experience as you passed over on dry ground?

On your third reading, go slowly and ask the Holy Spirit to help you think about the following experiences on this journey:

- everyone waiting three days before crossing over
- priests carrying the presence of God in the Ark of the Covenant
- priests going into the water first
- priests setting foot in the river and a dry path forming through the river
- priests standing (while still holding the Ark of the Covenant) in the middle of the river
- priest remaining (while still holding the Ark of the Covenant) in the river
- people crossing the river on dry ground
- God telling Joshua to choose twelve men, one from each tribe
- each tribe representative picking up a stone from where the priests were standing
- each tribe representative carrying a stone to the other side of the river
- Joshua commanding the priests to get out of the river
- priests stepping onto the other shore and the river waters returning to normal
- Joshua setting up the stones that were taken from the river
- Joshua coaching the Israelites on the meaning of the stones

Did the representative of your tribe contribute a stone? What is the power of the symbol? What will you tell your children when they ask what the boundary stones mean?

Do any of these real events in history resonate with symbolism in your life journey?

FOLLOWING THROUGH: Personalizing His promise

These chapters in Joshua are very early in biblical history. Perhaps the Promised Land of milk and honey wasn't everything that the Israelites and their physical and spiritual descendants hoped for. Nevertheless, God's covenantal promises are eternal. Arriving in Canaan was just a new beginning for His people.

Ponder what the Promised Land means in your life. Ask God to show you how He has and will continue to bring you to an ultimate place to be with Him. As you sense that He is doing that, consider how you will memorialize the journey.

XI

Inhabitation – *Walking Intentionally with God*

47

Walking in the Fear of the Lord

Does fear of the Lord mean the same thing as being afraid of God? Fear of the Lord shouldn't prompt you to hide, just the opposite. It should bring you face to face with the love of God.

Deuteronomy 10:12 (NIV 1984)

And now, O Israel, what does the LORD your God ask of you but to fear the LORD your God, to walk in all his ways, to love him, to serve the LORD your God with all your heart and with all your soul.

Deuteronomy 13:4 (NKJV)

You shall walk after the LORD your God and fear Him, and keep His commandments and obey His voice; you shall serve Him and hold fast to Him.

Psalm 25:12 (NLT)

Who are those who fear the LORD? He will show them the path they should choose.

Psalm 33:18 (NLT)

But the LORD watches over those who fear him, those who rely on his unfailing love.

Psalm 86:11 (NIV 1984)

Teach me your way, O LORD, and I will walk in your truth; give me an undivided heart, that I may fear your name.

Psalm 103:13 (NLT)

The LORD is like a father to his children, tender and compassionate to those who fear him.

Psalm 111:10 (NIV 1984)

The fear of the LORD is the beginning of wisdom; all who follow his precepts have good understanding. To him belongs eternal praise.

Psalm 145:18, 19 (NIV 1984)

The LORD is near to all who call on him, to all who call on him in truth. He fulfills the desires of those who fear him; he hears their cry and saves them.

Acts 9:31 (ESV)

So the church throughout all Judea and Galilee and Samaria had peace and was being built up. And walking in the fear of the Lord and in the comfort of the Holy Spirit, it multiplied.

ENTERING: Holding God's gaze

The audience has gone home, and the band has finished playing. The stage hands have left one stage light on. The singer is alone. She begins a solo, knowing God is listening. He is the only One who will review her work. Singing to an audience of One – that's "fear of the Lord." It is a way of living with the One who matters most watching.

The next day, the stage hands have everything up and running. The audience is back and the band is in full swing. The singer gives voice to her song once again. Again, in her heart, she sings for God alone. She hears only His applause.

From time to time, God may startle you. He who is bigger than the universe finds a way to show you that He cares about a small, seemingly insignificant detail of your life. Realizing His greatness – that is "fear of the Lord." He can humble you incredibly. Spend a moment pondering a sense of His extraordinary presence in an ordinary moment. Acknowledging Him then and there forms an inner attitude of expectation, an inner posture of prostration. That is "fear of the Lord"; it is the beginning of wisdom.

God's review is the one that counts the most in your life. He will bless you for singing, walking, and living this way. Hold the gaze of your loving Lord. He is worthy of your riveted reverence. Ask Him to steady your gaze on Him throughout this devotion so that you can sing with Him before you leave.

WALKING: Holding His hand

Ask Jesus to hold your hand as you walk through the scriptures. Imagine He alone speaks each verse to you. Think about the way "fear of the Lord" has been reframed for you. Stop after each verse and close your eyes. Keep your attention on this audience of One. Compose a personal paraphrase of what He is saying to you. Ask the Holy Spirit to add an insight from this verse or another. For example,

- From Deuteronomy 13, Jesus might say, "When you walk with Me and all your attention is on Me, you will be close enough to hear Me. What better way to understand your purpose in life and to make sure we don't come apart? Fearing Me is necessary."

- From Psalm 103, Jesus assures you, "You have a Father in heaven who cares deeply about your everyday struggles and efforts. When you fear Him, you can trust He has the upper hand in everything."

As you consider the verse from Acts, given what you have learned about God, how does "fear" combine with "comfort"? Spend a moment recalling an intense period of life when you walked with Jesus. Were you being persecuted for your faith in a God the world rejects? Or do you wonder why you have never been persecuted? Have you ever experienced this combination of "fear" and "comfort"?

Read through the verses one more time. Look at each one; decide if there is anything new, delightful, or surprising. Choose one verse to contemplate quietly. Stay in your contemplation until your heart is bowed in worship.

FOLLOWING THROUGH: Beholding Him

The power of praise is the power of God's presence. He isn't just on the receiving end; He inhabits the praise. He made the sound waves. He created musical scales. He created language. He endowed talent and loves those who abide in Him, skilled in singing or not. You are surrounded. Fear of the Lord… Let there be no one else in your heart but Him.

So praise Him with your heart bowed and feet tucked under. Behold the delight on His face for you. Continue beholding Him in praise.

And when you need to leave, notice the difference this praise and the fear of the Lord makes to the way you get up on your feet and the way you walk on.

48

Walking with God

In scripture, walking is a metaphor for relationship with God. Many Christians use this phrase without considering its deeper meaning. This devotion offers insight and instruction.

Genesis 5:24 (MSG)

Enoch walked steadily with God. And then one day he was simply gone: God took him.

Genesis 6:9 (NLT)

Noah was a righteous man, the only blameless person living on earth at the time, and he walked in close fellowship with God.

Genesis 17:1, 2 (NIV 1984)

When Abram was ninety-nine years old, the LORD appeared to him and said, "I am God Almighty; walk before me and be blameless. I will confirm my covenant between me and you and will greatly increase your numbers."

Leviticus 26:11–13 (MSG)

I'll set up my residence in your neighborhood; I won't avoid or shun you; I'll stroll through your streets. I'll be your God; you'll be my people. I am GOD, your personal God who rescued you from Egypt so that you would no longer be slaves to the Egyptians. I ripped off the harness of your slavery so that you can move about freely.

Isaiah 43:2 (NLT)

When you go through deep waters I will be with you. When you go through rivers of difficulty, you will not drown. When you walk through the fire of oppression, you will not be burned up; the flames will not consume you.

Micah 6:8b (NKJV)

What does the LORD require of you but to do justly, To love mercy, And to walk humbly with your God.

2 Corinthians 6:16 (NLT)

And what union can there be between God's temple and idols? For we are the temple of the living God. As God said, "I will live in them and walk among them. I will be their God, and they will be my people."

Matthew 11:29, 30 (MSG)

Walk with me and work with me – watch how I do it. Learn the unforced rhythms of grace. I won't lay anything heavy or ill-fitting on you. Keep company with me and you'll learn to live freely and lightly.

1 John 2:6 (NKJV)

He who says he abides in Him ought himself also to walk just as He walked.

ENTERING: Wearing the yoke

Jesus offers His yoke to you as you walk with Him. His contemporaries understood this agrarian image. A yoke was traditionally used to harness two working farm animals so that together they could pull or plough. The yoke was a heavy restraint on their movement. In Jesus' day, the yoke was also symbolic of the restrictions of slavery. He invited those who wore the enslaving yoke of the religious law to exchange it for His yoke, which would give them spiritual freedom.

The yoke of Christ is easy to wear and is lightweight. He guides your gait in a rhythm of restful reliance on Him. He wants to share your workload as you till the soil of unbelieving hearts and pull in the harvest of new believers. He models the walk of obedience to God the Father. He is your partner.

As you bow your head, think about what yoke is on your neck. Ask God for His.

WALKING: Talking the walk

Read the verses through once; ask the Holy Spirit to lead you. Underline phrases that instruct you on walking with God.

Next, identify three main themes:

- God's walking relationship with three spiritual forefathers
- God's commitment to walk with you, no matter how dire your circumstances
- God's revelation of how He sees you and what He needs from you

It is an old adage that the best way to learn something is to teach it. That being the case, you are going to instruct others on how to walk with God. Imagine that you are a Sunday school teacher or a trusted friend of a new believer. You have to explain what walking with God is all about. Find the verses that match these descriptions (or use your own words):

- The way we walk tells God and others a lot about us.
- God really knows you and has made it possible for you to walk without carrying the weight from bad memories.
- Walk with God every day; don't give up.
- Other people will want to walk with you when you walk with God.
- God teaches you how to walk with Him.
- God's reputation is on the line. It isn't just you doing the walking anymore.
- God changes you to be more like Jesus when you walk with Him.
- Share what you are worrying about or hoping for with God. Let Him know everything going on inside you.
- You are never alone, especially in the horrible times. God is getting you through to the other side.
- If you believe in Jesus, walk like He walked.

So, what did you learn for yourself? If you are near or just past a turning point in life, what do these verses mean to you now? Can you see that you are walking with God today? Bow your head so you can see your feet. Ask God for a blessing to be more conscious of them (and Him!) as you go in the same direction with Him today.

FOLLOWING THROUGH: Walking the talk

Copy the above list (and the verse references) on an index card or onto your smart phone. Highlight which one you want to remember over the near term. Carry the list with you. Highlight another characteristic of walking with God that strikes you on another day. Repeat this until you feel able to talk about what you are doing with other believers. Then try "talking the walk" with them.

49

Walking with the Holy Spirit

The trite expression "to walk and chew gum" refers to simultaneous activity on different levels of concentration. Walking with God's Spirit builds on this unconscious, innate ability. In fact, the Holy Spirit develops a walking and talking relationship within you that is both covert and compelling.

Luke 2:27, 28 (MSG)

The Holy Spirit had shown [Simeon] that he would see the Messiah of God before he died. Led by the Spirit, he entered the Temple. As the parents of the child Jesus brought him in to carry out the rituals of the Law, Simeon took him into his arms and blessed God.

Luke 4:1, 2a (NIV 1984)

Jesus, full of the Holy Spirit, returned from the Jordan and was led by the Spirit in the desert, where for forty days he was tempted by the devil.

John 20:20–22 (NLT)

As he spoke, he showed them the wounds in his hands and his side. They were filled with joy when they saw the Lord! Again he said, "Peace be with you. As the Father has sent me, so I am sending you." Then he breathed on them and said, "Receive the Holy Spirit."

Psalm 139:5, 7 (NLT)

You go before me and follow me. You place your hand of blessing on my head.... I can never escape from your Spirit! I can never get away from your presence!

Psalm 143:10 (NLT)

Teach me to do your will, for you are my God. May your gracious Spirit lead me forward on a firm footing.

Isaiah 30:21 (NLT)

Your own ears will hear him. Right behind you a voice will say, "This is the way you should go," whether to the right or to the left.

John 16:13 (NLT)

When the Spirit of truth comes, he will guide you into all truth. He will not speak on his own but will tell you what he has heard. He will tell you about the future.

Romans 8:1 (NKJV)

Those who are in Christ Jesus ... walk ... according to the Spirit.

Galatians 5:25 (NIV 1984)

Since we live by the Spirit, let us keep in step with the Spirit.

ENTERING: On-line

Telecommunications have changed the way you interact. Connected by an invisible web, you can blithely walk and text or talk to others unseen. For all of the outward changes, the principles of conversation remain the same. You send and receive, creating a feedback loop. How well does this analogy describe your communication with God?

The purpose of interacting with God hasn't changed since the beginning of time, but how it takes place has. Jesus' time on earth was the turning point. As a post-Pentecost Christian, you are mobile and on-line, walking and talking with His Holy Spirit, who dwells within you. In this feedback loop with God, sin can cause receptor problems. His attentive Spirit convicts you of a lapse; your confession clears the air waves. Communication resumes.

As you prepare to go through these scriptures, ask the Holy Spirit to clear your thoughts and to prepare your heart to receive His word.

WALKING: In tune

Read the first three verses slowly. They are examples of God divinely mobilizing people. In simple terms: He talks, you walk. If you face decisions or challenges, He helps you get through. He meets you where you are and enables your forward movement. Sometimes, out of nowhere it seems, He sends you out to do His will.

In this collection of scriptures you first walk through three critical points in the gospel account: Jesus' early childhood, the beginning of His ministry, and after His ascension. The Holy Spirit was active motivating hearts and moving feet

- identifying Jesus as the Messiah
- enabling Jesus to resist temptation
- taking up residence in Jesus' followers

These verses illustrate the Spirit's power to advance God's purposes through willing collaborators. He wants you to join Him in that. Reread John 20, and ask Jesus for the Holy Spirit.

Go slowly over the remaining verses; ask the Holy Spirit to show you His footwork. He is in you and all around you. In your inner spirit, you may have become accustomed to the sound of His footsteps in your day-to-day life. Reflecting on your life, how has the Spirit helped you make choices? Close your eyes and imagine His voice speaking into your heart. What draws you to him?

Read the scriptures again. Put yourself into Simeon's, Jesus', and then the disciples' sandals. Imagine that the Holy Spirit is speaking to each of them about their next steps as they journey on after those critical junctures.

- Simeon is on his way home.
- Jesus moves towards the cross.
- The disciples go out into the unwelcoming world.

They all must rely on the Spirit of God to lead them further. As they talk to God, they might borrow words from other verses in this devotion. Which verse might encourage Simeon the most? Which might speak strength into Jesus' heart? And which ones might the disciples memorize as they face the unknown? I think Simeon needs to hear Psalm 139; Jesus needs to hear Psalm 143; and the disciples need to hear Galatians 5. But what do you think?

Can you imagine these heavenly interactions as a feedback loop with communication initiated and received? Close your eyes and imagine the walking and talking, happening simultaneously, after a while with total ease. Now put yourself into the loop as you read the verses through one more time. What is the Holy Spirit saying to you? What do you want Him to say?

FOLLOWING THROUGH: In step

Look back at the verses that address you. Personalize the verses; declare each one as truth in your life. Write each one at the top of a page of a journal or on a piece of paper. Then pause and listen to the quiet inner voice of God's Spirit. As He leads you, continue the conversation in writing – confessing, praising, thanking, and asking for trust as He leads you onto the next steps of your life.

Return to these pages at a later date and add more of what you hear and what you need. Do you sense that you are getting to know the Holy Spirit better? Are you easing into step with Him?

50

Walking Tabernacles

You carry the presence of God when you walk. Your spiritual ancestors also carried His presence as they walked in the desert. God more than fulfilled His promise to walk with His people; He made His home with them, in them and in you. Trace the steps.

Tabernacle

Exodus 40:35b, 36 (NIV 1984)

The glory of the LORD filled the tabernacle. In all the travels of the Israelites, whenever the cloud lifted from above the tabernacle, they would set out.

Leviticus 26:11, 12 (NKJV)

I will set My tabernacle among you,… I will walk among you and be your God, and you shall be My people.

2 Samuel 7:6b (NLT)

[The Lord said] "I have always moved from one place to another with a tent and a Tabernacle as my dwelling."

Acts 7:44a (NLT)

"Our ancestors carried the Tabernacle with them through the wilderness. "

Temple

Acts 7:46a (NLT)

"David found favor with God and asked for the privilege of building a permanent Temple."

1 Kings 8:11b (NIV 1984)

The glory of the LORD filled his temple.

Haggai 2:9a (NLT)

The future glory of this Temple will be greater than its past glory, says the Lord of Heaven's Armies.

God Incarnate

John 1:14a (MSG)

The Word became flesh and blood, and moved into the neighborhood. We saw the glory with our own eyes, the one-of-a-kind glory, like Father, like Son.

Matthew 12:6 (NLT)

I tell you, there is one here who is even greater than the Temple!

Matthew 26:61 (NKJV)

"This fellow [Jesus] said, 'I am able to destroy the temple of God and to build it in three days.'"

Walking "Tabernacles"

1 Corinthians 6:19 (NIV 1984)

Do you not know that your body is a temple of the Holy Spirit, who is in you, whom you have received from God?

2 Corinthians 3:18 (NKJV)

But we all, with unveiled face, beholding as in a mirror the glory of the Lord, are being transformed into the same image from glory to glory, just as by the Spirit of the Lord.

2 Corinthians 6:16b, 17 (MSG)

Each of us [is] a temple in whom God lives. God himself put it this way: "I'll live in them, move into them; I'll be their God and they'll be my people."

ENTERING: Moving from place to place

Some homes are necessarily mobile. People depart on foot with the clothes on their backs. Think, for example, of refugees in Bosnia, Darfur, New Orleans, or Syria. Even though organizations advocate for their well-being, refugees live with uncertainty and degradation. Can you put yourself in their shoes?

Long before international policies on displaced persons, the Israelites were on the move. God orchestrated their release from captivity and manifestly led their travel on foot for 40 years. A portable sanctuary housed His presence, but the hovering cloud by day and the suspended fire at night assured them of His guidance. Can you put yourself in their shoes?

It is an archetype of human experience: walking in the desert toward the Promised Land. Transition may be the theme in your life too. This reflection walks us across the whole span of scripture, tracing how God kept His promise to walk very closely with His people. While you may not see footwork in every verse, each one describes the steps He took to assure His people of His presence. He puts Himself in the shoes of people on the move toward the Promised Land. Are you ready to put yours on?

WALKING: Moving from glory to glory

Ask the Holy Spirit to stay close. This collection of scriptures is sub-divided into four residences that God built for Himself. You are on a tour. You will learn why God transitioned from one to the other. He is also looking to find you a home. Chances are you could end up living with Him! You need a hard hat and steel-toed boots as you walk through this construction site. There is also some talk of demolition. Be alert: you will see important things and learn about things you cannot see.

First read through the scriptures to get an overview of the kinds of homes that God has chosen to dwell in.

- What do you think motivated His move from one home to the next?
- Which home was demolished? Any theory of why that happened? What replaced it?
- What role did mobility play in the new home that was "built" after the temple?
- What about the one after that?

On second reading, look for evidence that God was "at home." Typically, you know that someone is at home when the lights are on. Underline "glory" in all the sub-divisions. That's the sign that God is present. Just as you can't see the Holy Spirit, you cannot see glory. The

Spirit is often symbolized as wind or breath, which you can see only in its effects on you or your surroundings. Glory is like that. It was often depicted as a cloud. What happens when God's glory inhabits each of His homes?

On third reading, revisit all the verses, praising God with this psalm: "I love the house where you live, O LORD, the place where your glory dwells" (Psalm 26:8, NIV 1984).

Are you ready to move in and on with God?

FOLLOWING THROUGH: Moving in His name

Pull out your Bible and ponder two more verses that illuminate God's house moving and your place in His home:

- God still needs a mobile home. You are His "walking tabernacle." See Acts 1:8
- God has a final move in mind. He wants you with Him. Check out Revelation 21:22.

Finally, take a deep breath. Ask God to help you understand the reality of the presence and glory of God as close as your heart beat. God keeps His promises; He is right there with you.

Appendix

Table of Contents ... Cross-referenced to Chapter Introductions

Invitation to "Follow Me" – *Responding to God's Love*

1. Finding God's Path

In trying to find a way forward in life, you naturally ask others about paths they have traveled. The path metaphor in the Bible depicts a close relationship with God through all of life's circumstances.

2. Following Jesus

When Jesus called the disciples, they got up on their feet and left their jobs; they literally followed Him. They soon learned that following was a synchronized motion of heart and feet.

3. Running the Race

For St. Paul, running the race is a metaphor for life: getting in, staying in, finishing and winning. He is not a lone runner; he has a role for you on his team.

4. Running with the Message

When you receive a message that is true and life-changing, you probably feel compelled to tell others. Your feet get moving and spreading the message gains momentum.

5. Walking in His Ways

The way God wants you to walk is how He defines His character. Would you say the same for yourself?

Transformation in One Step - *Pivoting to God's Presence*

6. Arise!

The motion of rising on your feet in response to God's command is a picture of resurrection. In scripture, rising up is a sign that God has something new under way. In these passages I have added emphasis on the pertinent terms.

7. Returning to God

You may be watching and waiting for a wayward child to return home. The parable of the prodigal son helps you listen to God's emphatic promises to that child.

8. Turning to God

Toe-to-toe and face-to-face with God is where He wants to be with you. Check your feet and consider turning to Him from where you are right now.

9. Walking from Darkness to Light

Just as your physical senses attune to changes in the environment, your ears and eyes adjust as you approach God's presence. Metaphors of light and dark direct your footwork in this spiritual experience.

Coordination of Faith and Feet – *Experiencing God's Strength*

10. Heart and Soles

Piano students often learn to play the duet called "Heart and Soul" as a first experience of coordinating with another player. Accompaniment is a musical metaphor of how God coordinates His heart with yours. "Heart and Soles" is word play revealing how God orchestrates your walk with Him.

11. The Prime Mover

The expression "let go and let God" declares that God can do what you cannot. In this devotion, you contemplate God as the source of your strength, and the one who enables you to move forward.

12. Standing Firm

Standing firmly in one place is difficult. Physically, pain and impatience vie for your attention. Spiritually, your enemy mistakes your stability for inability. He's wrong: standing firmly is a still-life representation of animate faith. Sometimes, in your spiritual walk, standing is the strongest position you can take.

13. Walking in Obedience

God commands that you walk in obedience to Him but He never insists on it. In this devotion, you explore how to make His commands for your feet the desire of your heart.

Protection and Foot Care– *Receiving God's Touch*

14. Foot Coverings

Shoes tell stories about the wearer. The footwear of a ballerina, a welder or a nurse are each distinct; shoes symbolize stories of the life lived in them. Between the lines is a spiritual narrative: God designed foot coverings to tell His story.

15. Foot Washing

In picking up a towel and a basin to wash their feet, Jesus took on the role of servant to His disciples. Through foot-washing, the disciples discovered that they had a lot to learn about the depth of Jesus' servant love for them.

16. Guarding your Feet

When you walk with God, you can rest assured that He 'has' your feet. Your challenge is to remember that no matter where you go.

17. The Lame Walk

One of the most beautiful images of Jesus extending love on earth is in His healing of the lame. The Old Testament associates this healing with the restoration of relationship. Jesus didn't disagree.

18. Miracles on Foot

Among the many spiritual influences in society, are those which emphasize the physical universe above the One who created it. This devotion offers snippets of stories about human feet encountering the Creator's power. These miracles declare who rightly deserves your worship.

19. Rescuing your Feet

Through prayer, God can repair any brokenness. You may not think of your feet or footwork as broken but God does. He created them to be fully-functioning for His glory and they aren't. He has given you His word that He will rescue them.

Direction on the Road – *Experiencing God's Leadership*

20. Companions on the Road

Caution: walking with others is a test of care, comfort and credibility. It is a two-way street; companions can influence each other positively and negatively.

21. Detours

It is a rare life that stays a steady course. God uses unexpected turns to challenge you. Your feet adapt to different terrain and to round-about routes. You discover that you need Him along the way and that He has arranged every step you took.

22. Guiding your Feet

The guidance God gives your feet are foundational to all of life's decisions and directions. He wants you to ask Him for it.

23. Marches and Processions

Think of the messages that feet deliver: goose-stepping soldiers – taunting. The Million Man March – daunting. When God leads the march, His message is triumph – yours, in Christ.

24. The Road to Emmaus

Emotions can affect your awareness of what is happening around you. On the road to Emmaus, two downcast disciples were so focused on a past experience that they barely noticed their feet move forward. In this devotion, you reflect on what is preventing you from seeing Jesus in your spiritual walk.

25. Road Signs

Signs direct you to destinations and warn of hazards or changes in road conditions. What is true in the material world is true in the spiritual. God's signs give us a sense of the spiritual conditions of the road ahead of us.

26. Wise Moves

As you go through life, you accumulate wisdom. Sometimes, you need fresh wisdom. Other times you need to reassess what you have before you go forward.

Distractions and Obstructions – *Avoiding the Pitfalls*

27. Entrapment

Be alert to the ground game in spiritual conflict. Be aware that God goes on the offence when your feet are trapped.

28. Following other Gods

God warns wayward feet that follow other gods. This wrong move has big consequences.

29. Footholds

Have you ever heard the expression, "Don't let the enemy get a foothold."? If you are a follower of Jesus, then God's work is to secure His foothold in your life.

30. Self-inflicted Traps

Feet and footwork are good indicators on how your life is going. If you walk freely and safely, that's wonderful. There are metaphors that describe the opposite: traps, snares, ambushes, and pits. Some of these are of your own making.

31. Stumbling, Tripping and Falling

If you don't pay attention to your feet, you can suddenly stumble, trip and even fall. Walking often entails consciously going around or over obstacles. In this devotion, you reflect on paying attention to your spiritual footwork.

32. Turning away from God

When you take one step away from God, it is a significant move. Your heart dictates the decision. Your feet follow your heart, taking you in another direction.

33. Walking in Darkness

The sheer number of verses in this Passage stress how crucial this topic is to God. His truth cannot be concealed.

34. Wandering

In this devotion, you will reflect on loved ones who have wandered from their spiritual home or their family home, or possibly both. As part of the exercise, you will have an opportunity to write a love letter to the wanderer you are missing.

35. Wrong Moves

Have you ever felt the power of persuasion to the point where you couldn't resist? Giving up your will is not God's will.

Devotion on Holy Ground – *Walking in God's Power*

36. At His Feet

In ancient days, people sat at the feet of their teachers. Those at Jesus' feet could testify to His divine interventions on their behalf.

37. Barefoot on Holy Ground

In this devotion, you reflect on encounters with God, through the story of Moses and the burning bush.

38. Footstool of God

God lives in your heart. The concept of God's footstool invites you to visualize that He is at home there, resting His feet and bidding you to approach.

39. God's Feet

The Bible often depicts God as having physical qualities –including having feet. In this devotion, glimpses of His feet portray how supernatural He is.

40. Taking Territory

Walking with God accomplishes His purposes to transform your life. Through you, He also transforms your community and the very land you walk on.

41. Under God's Feet

Some footwork metaphors in the Bible portray God as warrior and victor. He is, after all, the Lord of Heaven's Armies. This devotion helps you understand what He is fighting for.

42. Under Your Feet

In this devotion, we look at the notion of trampling enemies underfoot as an invitation to focused prayer.

Destination – *Following Jesus beyond the Narrow Gate*

43. Entering God's Kingdom

The footwork of entering is a single step, preceded and followed by other steps. But the foot that crosses a threshold declares 'entry accomplished.' And so it is, when you enter the Kingdom of God.

44. Entering the Most Holy Place

This footwork metaphor deepens understanding of how it is possible for you to follow an ascended Savior from an earthly walk to a heavenly home. "On earth, as it is in heaven" is a prayer answered.

45. Standing in God's Presence

Qualifying to stand in God's presence requires meeting the highest standard of holiness. This devotion asks, "Who may stand?" and "On what basis?"

46. Standing in the Promised Land

An immigrant might kiss the ground of a new homeland. The Israelites marked their gratitude by standing on the boundary in the presence of God. Later, they honored the memory with stones from that unusual place.

Inhabitation – *Walking Intentionally with God*

47. Walking in the Fear of the Lord

Does fear of the Lord mean the same thing as being afraid of God? Fear of the Lord shouldn't prompt you to hide, just the opposite. It should bring you face to face with the love of God.

48. Walking with God

In scripture, walking is a metaphor for relationship with God. Many Christians use this phrase without considering its deeper meaning. This devotion offers insight and instruction.

49. Walking with the Holy Spirit

The trite expression 'to walk and chew gum' refers to simultaneous activity on different levels of concentration. Walking with God's Spirit builds on this unconscious, innate ability. In fact, the Holy

Spirit develops a walking and talking relationship within you that is both covert and compelling.

50. Walking Tabernacles

You carry the presence of God when you walk. Your spiritual ancestors also carried His presence as they walked in the desert. God more than fulfilled His promise to walk with His people; He made His home with them, in them and in you. Trace the steps.